P9-BIL-486

9.14.78

THE
IRRESISTIBLE
AMERICAN
SOFTBALL
BOOK

THE IRRESISTIBLE AMERICAN SOFTBALL BOOK

by Edward Claflin

DOLPHIN BOOKS

Doubleday & Company, Inc.

GARDEN CITY, NEW YORK   1978

PICTURE CREDITS

Grateful acknowledgment is made to the following people for permission to use the illustrations and photographs that appear in this book.

For his cartoons: Pete Kalberkamp (pages 7, 36, 63, 70, 98, 118, 119, 120, 121, and 121).

For her sketches: Ellen Foote (pages 39, 40, 40, 42, 43, 43, and 44).

For their photographs: Robin Platzer (pages xiv and 56); Darlene Watson (pages 2, 26, 27, 28, 72, 73, 74, and 124); Collection of Lowell Thomas (pages 4, 100, 101, 103, and 104); The Chicago Historical Society (page 6); United Press International (pages 11 and 76); Berny H. Friewall and the Historical Society of Forest Park, Illinois (page 15); Jerome Earnest, *Super Slowpitch:* (pages 16 and 48); George Linnehan (pages 21 and 23); Edward Claflin (pages 30, 53, 64, and 93); William Kuebler (page 54); Walter Stricklin (page 60); Joan E. Chandler (page 68); Sunday *Post:* (page 70); Eddie Feigner (pages 82 and 84); Royal Beaird (page 86); Howard C. O'Reilly (page 89); Clyde Fairfield (page 90); The Kids and Kubs (page 91); Fran Lewin (page 95); Ken Hawkins/Sygma (page 97); Amateur Softball Association (pages 108, 109, 110, 111, 112, 113, 114, 115, 115, 116, 116, and 117); Meg Gage (page 29).

A Dolphin Books Original
Doubleday & Company, Inc.

Library of Congress Cataloging in Publication Data

Claflin, Edward.
    The irresistible American softball book.

    1. Softball.   2. Softball—Anecdotes, facetiae, satire, etc.   I. Title.
GV881.C55   796.357′8′0207
ISBN: 0-385-13053-8
Library of Congress Catalog Card Number 77–12845

To John B. Warthen
on first

ACKNOWLEDGMENTS

Lindy Hess, bless her, said, "How about a softball book?" and forthwith granted the support of Doubleday. John B. Warthen grinned and got me started with about ten pages of notes. Johnny Moon, in Atlanta, gave me a precious paperbound copy of Morris A. Bealle's *Softball Story*. Doc Linnehan sketched the history of the County Sports-turned-Pepsico team and reviewed the instructions for pitching and hitting. Frank Ancona introduced me to the softballers in the Concentrate Division at Pepsico. Don Porter and Dave Hill contributed definitive material from the Amateur Softball Association. Ken Ruffo, Oscar Steadman, and Ray Molphy told me what it's like to see and play softball among hotshots. Jim Jensen invited me to ride the bus with the WCBS All-Stars. John Pinero, Nelson Alvarez, and Lee Otis introduced me to the Central Park men's leagues. Fran Lewin contributed the complete history of the Broadway Show League. Gaylen Savage and Bob Vassil steered me to the indomitable J. C. Penney women's team. Bill Plummer of the ASA threw out some encouragement, then followed up with suggestions and clippings. Andrew French told me about the Regulars. Al Lewis of the Raybestos Cardinals patiently demonstrated the fast pitch . . . and, oh my, the list could go on and on.

Beryl Loeb cheered for softball and kept it rolling through draft after draft. Pete Kalberkamp produced a bunch of softball cartoons that you won't forget. Ellen Foote did the elegant sketches found in Chapter 3, and Darlene Watson braved the dust and heat of midsummer to take photographs of Central Park teams and players.

What a team! I'd like to give everyone a six-foot trophy with "Thanks" in gold leaf.

If you are a softball scoffer, try playing it.
Then if you don't like it, try having your head examined.
—from *Softball: So What?*
by Lowell Thomas and Ted Shane

CONTENTS

THE IRRESISTIBLE AMERICAN SOFTBALL BOOK

Al Pacino, star shortstop for the *Pavlo Hummel* softball team in the Broadway Show League. He's grinning like a kid 'cause he just made the third out.

Chapter 1

SOFTBALL POWER

A NATIONAL ADDICTION

Or call it an obsession. Call it infectious, habit-forming, irresistible, call it what you will, it's the most popular team sport in the United States. Good old softball.

You'll see the early symptoms in springtime, when the grass isn't quite green, but getting there, and the morning breeze still has some bite to it, but who cares—you won't even notice after you've been running around for a couple of minutes. Springtime, and the big leagues are setting their baseball teams for the season, and the free agents are making up their minds, and the final contracts are being signed for pitchers, catchers, infielders, and outfielders who are going for six- or seven-digit figures in the American and National Leagues. They've gone South for spring training, and the sports section reports how the Pirates did better than expected in pre-season games, the Braves did worse, and the Yankees no better or worse than they had to.

But for about thirty million people, spring means something besides the big baseball contracts and Florida training and sports-page scuttle butt. Spring means softball. And softball isn't something you read about or sit and watch. Softball is something you do.

In bars and cafes, warehouses, factories, in small town and large metropolitan recreation areas, in law offices and architect firms and trucking companies, in schools and churches and real estate offices, in the Pentagon and the House of Representatives, in restaurants and hamburger joints, in brewing companies and accounting firms, in the FBI and the Elks and the VFW, at the corner gas station and the second-hand Ford dealer, and in pizza parlors and tire shops and tool companies, in suburban neighborhoods and in city streets, they're getting ready to play softball.

The glove comes out of the closet. Last year's ball is found, still wearing a faint green stain. Hands large and small, male and female, tough and soft put brand-new bats to the test. Swinging them slowly. Then faster. Dreaming. An imagined ball floats toward you, toward an imagined plate. There's the windup, the step, the swing, and an invisible ball reverses direction, soaring obediently toward the horizon of an imagined fence.

In 1976 there were at least 26 million players in the United States and 35 million worldwide. The Amateur Softball Association

Moms, dads, kids, and chums turn out for Sunday softball games *à la* barbecue and picnic in the park. They're all part of the softball boom.

of the United States—the largest, but by no means the only such organization—found in 1976 that there were 17,471,000 players on *organized* teams: 77,000 teams in the ASA, 275,000 in public recreation, 35,000 teams playing for 4,930 companies in industrial leagues, with 9,000,000 children playing in 56,100 public and private schools, and 25,000 teams in the armed forces. Softball is now ranked as the largest team-participation sport in the United States.

Not baseball? Oh, no, no, no! You see, baseball, these days, is for the few. Softball is for the many.

There are a number of obvious differences between baseball and softball. The baseball

has a 9-inch circumference, and most softballs are 12 inches around. (There are also 14-inch and 16-inch softballs, but the 12-inch variety is by far the most popular.) The softball isn't really softer, since it's made of essentially the same materials as a baseball—a dense cork center surrounded by a rubber binder, wound with yarn, and covered with leather. (Cheaper versions are covered with rubber or synthetic material.) Anyone who's ever been stung in the thigh by a softball knows the blasted thing is every bit as hard as a baseball. He'll tell you so, when he stops yowling.

In softball the pitch is always underhand. In the early days of baseball, all the pitchers used an underhand throw, but in about 1884, for unexplained reasons, baseballers switched to the overhand. The softball pitch allows for as much or more variety as the baseball throw. It can be a slow sort of lob ball; or it can come in at medium speed and do some contortions such as curve, rise, or drop; or it can be pitched with blazing speed.

The base lines and the distance from the pitcher's mound to home plate are shorter in softball than in baseball, and softball games go for seven innings as opposed to baseball's nine. The distance between bases is set at 60 feet (compared to 90 feet in baseball), and the pitcher is only 46 feet away from the batter in softball (less for women's fast pitch), while he stands 60½ feet away in baseball. The distance to the fence varies from one field to the next, but most of the softball fields have a shorter home-run fence than major league baseball stadiums.

Of course, if you're playing softball and just using your brother's jacket as a home-run mark, you can put it anywhere you like. And move it out thirty yards or so when *he* comes to bat.

In effect, the short base lines create a faster game. A fast pitch seems to cross the plate almost the same instant it leaves the pitcher's hand. In a play on first, the action is much faster, since both the runner and the ball are covering less ground. Since the game goes only seven innings, it's shorter than a comparable baseball game. Frequently a softball game takes no more than an hour or an hour-and-a-half to play—so you can fit several games into an afternoon.

There are basically two kinds of softball —slow pitch and fast pitch. When the sport started, fast pitch was by far the more popular game. The pitcher could throw at any speed, and almost any kind of windup was allowed. A fast ball, thrown underhand, travels at about 90 miles per hour, and a powerful pitcher can get it over the plate at 100 or 110 mph—as fast as any baseball. Rules for bunting and stealing are generally the same in fast pitch as they are in baseball.

In slow pitch, the windup and toss are restricted to insure that the ball comes over the plate at a dignified pace. According to 1977 rules, the ball has to describe an arc more than 3 feet above the point where the pitcher releases the ball but not more than 12 feet above the ground. No stealing or bunting are allowed in slow pitch, and there is a tenth man, a "shortfielder" in the outfield. In slow pitch, the batter naturally has a much better chance of slugging the ball.

In recent years the popularity of fast pitch has declined, until today about 80 per cent of the teams in the United States are playing slow pitch. Fast pitch remains popular in many women's leagues, but the majority of players prefer a safer game where hitting and fielding are more important than pitching. The speed of the pitch makes an obvious difference in the pace of the game. Fast-pitch softball is dominated by the pitcher, and if the person on the mound is an ace with a hot fast ball, a curve, knuckler, rise and drop, well, it's not much fun playing right field. You might as well go home and eat your Cracker Jacks because you'll probably go a whole game without getting a hand on the ball. For everyone but the pitcher, the afternoon of free recreation may turn into a big yawn.

In slow pitch, where there's more hitting, you're guaranteed more infield and outfield play—in total, a much more action-packed game for the whole team. For me in particular, it's a chance to make more errors than I ever dreamed possible.

One of the most virtuous aspects of softball history—both slow and fast pitch—is that women have always played the game and always will. Girls are still a novelty among Little League baseball teams, but girls have always held equal turf in softball. During the thirties and forties, women's softball drew larger

Slow pitch or fast—it all depended on the mood of the pitcher in the early days of softball. Batter is Colonel Teddy Roosevelt. Scene: Pawling, New York, in the 1930s.

crowds than men's, and today the women's fast-pitch softball leagues have some of the best female athletes in the country.

In the rule book, the pitching distance is shortened to 40 feet for women's fast pitch, and the fence is a minimum of 250 feet in women's slow pitch, instead of the men's minimum of 275 feet. (In fast pitch, the minimum is 225 feet for both men and women.) Otherwise, we find no signs of concession, and anyone who has seen a women's pro pitcher tossing the ball at 95 miles per hour will think twice and duck three times before talking about the weaker sex.

There are, however, a few sexist ghosts that lurk unbidden in the chambers of this sport. For one thing, while there are numerous women's teams in championship play, there are no mixed teams—the "separate but equal" clause is still enforced everywhere but on a

few playground, recreation, and choose-up teams. It's rare, also, to find an all-male team playing an all-female team in serious competition, though numerous matches have been set for exhibition games of this kind—as if it were some kind of spectacle to see the war between the sexes enacted on the diamond.

Another curious aspect of women's softball (frequently and innocently called "girls" or "gals" softball by you-know-who) is that female teams frequently have male managers. Maybe this is because male sponsors have in the past put their bucks behind a team—but there seems to be the blatant assumption that men should be managers, even after all these generations of women playing top-notch ball, because the "fellas" should show the "gals" how to do it. Enough of that.

As for the stereotype of the woman softball player as a big, brawny, unfeminine Amazon—forget it. Female players come in all shapes and sizes, and besides, you shouldn't indulge in stereotypes.

In softball of all varieties, it is traditional to derive the name of the team from the name of the sponsor, but if you don't have a sponsor, the sprightly results of an overheated imagination will do. And oh what names there be. There's Sportsprint Saints, Bertuca Bonding, McLoone Metal Graphics, and the Unwanted Lighthouse of Baneld, Illinois. Razorbach Concrete, Tri-State Auction, the Coffeen Roadrunners, and the Tucson Cactus Room. Chicago gives us the Amalgamonsters and the Flamingos. Fairfield, California, is proud to present Vinatieri Roofing, while Tarpon Springs, Florida, features the Spongerettes. The Federal Aviation Administration from Memphis has in times past fallen to Louisville Gas and Electric but kept its lead over Hutzel Hospital of Detroit. When the prayers are over, Hickory Hammock Baptist will still have a one-game lead over Grace Methodist and Burke Road Church of Christ, and the Central Assembly won't lose to Lafayette Nazarene until judgment day comes again. History is full of them, these unabashed name-dropping softballers. Idaho had Boise's Baird Cleaners, Kuna's Girls Club, and Kenny Poe's Plumbers. Illinois matched the Champagne Velvets against Litzinger Motors, and California made history with its Hollister Cowboys, Hammer Airfield, Western Gravel, and Krieg's Haberdashery. And, as the saying goes, behind every name is a story.

WHO'S TO BLAME?

The man most often accused of starting the softball epidemic was George W. Hancock, a reporter for the Chicago Board of Trade, who came up with the first set of usable rules in 1887. The National League was already about ten years old, and everyone knew about baseball, but they had never tried playing it indoors. On Thanksgiving Day George Hancock and a group of alumnae from Harvard and Yale were at the Farragut Boat Club on Lake Park Avenue, waiting to hear the results from the Yale-Harvard football game. At last the scores came in, and the Harvard men got out their wallets to pay off their bets. Yale had won, 17–8.

But the real game was just about to begin. It might have been Tom Jenkins, a dry goods merchant, Lyman Glover, a theater manager, or Edwin Anderson, a superintendent of the Boat Club—*someone* got out a boxing glove, used the laces to tie it into a mushy sort of cannonball, and began tossing it around the room. Someone else picked up a broom handle and said, "Here, pitch me one." And George Hancock said, "Hey, what about a game of baseball?"

Well, it was too cold and windy to go outside, so Harvard men played the Yalies in the exercise room of the Boat Club. They marked out lines on the floor with a piece of chalk, marked bases on the wrestling mat, and whacked the ball around until the score was about 41–40. Later on, George Hancock

The Farragut Boat Club in Chicago. It was in an exercise room of this building that the first game of softball was played by Ivy Leaguers.

made up some Club rules for the game, and the Ivy Leaguers played all winter long.

Then the mania spread. In *The Softball Story* (1957), Morris A. Bealle described the turn of events that followed as one city after another took up the game. According to Bealle, softball appeared next in Minneapolis.

In 1895 a fireman with the Minneapolis Fire Co. No. 11, Lieutenant Lewis Rober, Sr., started playing softball in the vacant lot next to the firehouse. No one knows whether he had heard about Hancock's version, or whether Rober just adapted baseball to suit his own purposes, but it turned out to be a habit-forming recreation for the Minneapolis

firemen. In the '90s the firemen were on call twenty-four hours a day. They lived on the second floor of the station house and commuted to work on a brass pole. They'd resort to anything, absolutely anything, to fill the time. Lieutenant Rober had promoted boxing matches as a way to keep the men occupied, and in his spare time he had put together medicine balls—large, leather-covered balls that were good for a game of catch.

A medicine ball became his first softball. Rober cleared the stones from the vacant lot next door and marked out a diamond that was half the size of a baseball diamond, with a pitching distance of 35 feet. A wood turner made a bat with a 2-inch diameter, and the firemen's franchise was in business. Other fire companies joined the league a few weeks later, and it spread to the city's playgrounds, where perfectly innocent children were exposed to the ravages of the epidemic.

The next year, 1896, Rober was transferred to Fire Company No. 19, where he organized a team called the Kittens. The Kittens were promptly challenged by the Rats of Engine Co. 9, who practiced in a secretive and rodent-like manner to pull the whiskers off Rober's company. According to the record, the Kittens won the first game, 5–0, and the Rats scurried away with the second, 4–2. A crowd of 1,500 showed up on two successive Saturday afternoons to see the games.

By 1900 there was a full-fledged league made up of the Kittens of Engine House 19, the Rats of No. 9, the Whales of No. 4, plus playground teams called the Salisburys, the Pillsburys, and the Central Avenues. Frequently, the games were watched by crowds of 3,000 or more, and there was intense partisanship. According to the Chicago *Tribune*, the situation in town began to resemble all-out civil war. "Sometimes two brothers would belong to two different teams," wrote one reporter. "Spirit would be so intense that families would be divided on the merits of the two teams, and some members of a family would go a whole season without speaking to one another."

Although the sport spread from house to house and block to block, creating dissension and unrest everywhere, no one knew what to call it. It wasn't until 1900 that Captain George Kehoe of Truck Company No. 1 came up with the name Kitten League Ball (later shortened to Kitten Ball) in honor of Lieutenant Rober's original squad. In 1913 the game was officially adopted by the Park Board of Minneapolis, and by 1915 it had swept St. Paul, where it was described (in the *Pioneer Press*) as "an ideal after-dinner sport which may be indulged in by any person, man or woman, without danger of injury or lameness." Noting that there were nine new leagues in St. Paul, the *Press* observed, "Wherever there is a playground or a plot of ground large enough to lay out a diamond, there the Kitten game will be found."

Within a few years, the game had spread to every part of the country, urged on by Park Department officials who thought it was the greatest athletic invention of the century. It traveled under a variety of disguises. The name Kitten Ball dropped out about 1922, and after that it was called Mush Ball, Diamond Ball, Playground Ball, Pumpkin Ball, Recreation Ball, Big Ball, Twilight Ball,

Ridge Ball, Army Ball, Indoor Ball (or Indoor-Outdoor), Lightning Ball, Sissy Ball and Dainty Drawers. But the name that finally stuck, Softball, is slightly ridiculous since the ball isn't soft. Credit is generally given to Walter L. Hakanson of the Denver, Colorado, YMCA, for introducing the misnomer in 1926 at an organizational meeting in Chicago.

It required innumerable organizational meetings to straighten out the confusion of softball rules, since each part of the country had come up with its own version of the game. The indoor diamond, originally with a base line of 27 feet, was arbitrarily enlarged to 30, 35, and 40 feet. And the distance of the pitcher's box from home plate (30–46 feet) depended on the state you were in, the size of the field, the mood of the players, and the mental aptitude of the gentleman who marked out the field.

One early set of rules adapted in 1908 by the National Amateur Playground Association of the United States allowed the team to play five, seven, or nine innings, with the option of reverse baserunning and a point system of scoring. Playing by these rules, the first batter to get a hit each inning could run to either first base or third base. If he ran to third all the following batters had to run the bases in that order for the rest of the inning. Also the teams could score by points instead of runs, allowing one point each time a runner reached a base. After struggling with these bizarre rules for a number of years, the organizers realized that something had to be done.

GETTING IT TOGETHER

The first interstate organization that tried to straighten out this mess was the National Diamond Ball Association, founded in 1925 in Minneapolis by Harold A. Johnson, assistant director of recreation for the Minneapolis Park Board. Back in 1916 Mr. Johnson had made a four-month study of baseball, kittenball, and indoor baseball, then published his own set of rules for the game and standards for equipment. He convinced the Minneapolis merchants that they should sponsor four teams, and he held a city-wide name-the-sport contest to help him decide what to call the creation. There were three hundred names submitted, and Mr. Johnson chose Diamond Ball.

Within a few years, the infant Diamond Ball League had 828 teams, and seven baseball diamonds in the Minneapolis Parade Ground were converted to twenty-four softball diamonds. After the twin city of St. Paul started its own Diamond Ball League, the rage spread to the neighboring states of Wisconsin, North Dakota, South Dakota, Iowa, and to the province of Winnipeg, Canada. The first Twin-City Tournament was held in 1918, and by 1925 there were men's, women's, junior's and midget leagues competing for the Twin-City title. Margaret Bluffers of St. Paul beat the Non-XL's of Minneapolis in two out of three games, and became the first women's champion in the Northwest area. The same year, the Bertsches of Minneapolis defeated the Red Crowns in the final, and the Logan Park kids (who were hot that year) swept the junior and midget leagues. By 1927 the National Diamond Ball Association was holding state-wide tournaments. In the first year Bubbles Cafe of St. Paul smashed Dinty Moore's of St. Cloud, 7–0 in the final game.

In 1932 the national championship tournament included forty teams from six states, with Wisconsin winning the first four places, in the following order: Wemcoes (Lake Mills), Miller High Life (Kenosha), Peck and Sons (Milwaukee), and Three Aces (Kenosha). Other teams from Wisconsin included the Jesch-Schafers, Black Bears, Western Printers, Bluejays, Modern Laundry, Racine Transfer and Storage, Golden Drops, Jaeger Bakeries, All Stars, Bodegas, Cardinals, Menominee Falls, Lithias, Winter Clothiers, Hunkel Seeds, Hootkin Grocers, Square Deal Food Shops, Curley's Tavern, Plymouth Creamery, and Schlitz Brewery, may their names long be remembered.

After this season Mr. Johnson left softball to enter the ministry and became the pastor of Trinity Lutheran Church in Enumclaw, Washington. Apparently, he needed a change of pace.

A new and more powerful organization, the Amateur Softball Association of America, was started in Chicago the following year, 1933, with the backing of William Randolph Hearst's newspaper, the Chicago *American*. A sportswriter for the *American,* Leo Fischer, suggested that the newspaper sponsor and promote a nationwide softball tournament as part of the 1933 Chicago World's Fair. The Hearst General Promotion Department in New York liked the idea, and saw the opportunity to promote the sport nationwide through the twenty-four newspapers owned by the Hearst Corporation. Michael J. Pauley, a sporting goods salesman, was chosen to help Fischer recruit teams. Fischer got in the family car and headed West, while Pauley went East, and after ten days they had found forty men's and ten women's teams willing to come to Chicago for the extravaganza. Fischer and a sports promotion director, Harry D. Wilson, chose another sixteen men's and eight women's teams from the Chicago area—and arranged to use the fair grounds at the Century of Progress Exposition, with seating for thousands of spectators. There were separate divisions for fast pitch, slow pitch, and women, and the 14-inch ball was used for all games.

Seventy thousand spectators attended the first championship games, and the Chicago *American* called it the "largest and most comprehensive tournament ever held in the sport which has swept the country like wildfire." In the fast-pitch division, J. J. Gillis of Chicago beat Briggs Bodyworks, 5–0, in the final. The Chicago team, Great Northerns, defeated Roby Playground, Downer's Grove, and Chase Park to take the women's title. In slow pitch, Cuyler Missions beat Forest Park, 10–3, in the semifinals and snatched the championship with a 10–4 win over Cinderella Florists.

After the World's Fair Tournament, Leo Fischer met with visiting officials of other organizations to form a Joint Rules Committee, which would develop unified softball rules, and the Amateur Softball Association grew out of these meetings. Leo Fischer became the first president of the ASA with Mike Pauley as executive secretary and treasurer, and during the next few years the Hearst organization provided some $50,000 in financial backing for softball tournaments.

HOW ORGANIZED CAN YOU GET?

In 1976 the Amateur Softball Association registered 1,771,000 members with 67,000 adult and 10,000 junior teams. At present the Association has separate divisions for men's and women's fast pitch—with "major leagues" playing top ball and an "A" division for teams in a lower category. There are girls' leagues and boys' leagues for ages 9–12, 13–15, and 16–18, plus separate divisions for major industrial slow pitch, major 16-inch slow pitch, church slow pitch, and modified pitch. In the mind of each and every ASA commissioner, this nation of ours is divided into fifteen regions, and the weekends between April and September are tidy bundles of district, state, metropolitan, regional, and national tournaments.

Tournaments last three or four days, with as many as fifty or sixty teams clambering for the position of national champs. If it starts to rain, the teams just play between cloudbursts. Thunderstorms, hailstorms, and generally nasty weather seem to be traditional on tournament weekends, and these ASA softballers are more or less resigned to it. If the weather clears up at 2 A.M. in the morning, they'll go out and play at 2 A.M. If that means playing five games in a row on Sunday night, they'll play five games in a row. On a tournament weekend, anything goes.

Naturally, the tournaments draw thousands of spectators. Families arrive in campers, trailers, tents, and caravans and just set up camp for the weekend. It's quite a sight, late in the evening, to see the campfires glowing out there beyond right field. While Dubois Chemical beats Beef Corral, Dad grills the hamburgers and Mom puts the kids to bed, and then they come right back to the stands to watch for the rest of the night. Oh yes, there's also beer—lots of it—and the crunch of aluminum underfoot.

As for the local motels, they do a booming business. Most softball sponsors get first-class accommodations for their teams, and Chambers of Commerce all over the country are more than happy to welcome these hordes of fanatic softballers to their towns for the weekend. Tournaments are judiciously scattered around the country by agreement of the ASA Commissioners' Council, and locations change from year to year.

The headquarters of the ASA is in Oklahoma City, where a gleaming new Hall of Fame has indirect lighting, waxwork figures in softball uniforms, and a complete reference library—including doctoral dissertations on the sport of softball. In addition to the staff at the national office, there is a spiderlike corporate structure consisting of some hundred state and metropolitan commissioners under nine vice-presidents and 2,500 voluntary district and deputy commissioners. The ASA is affiliated with the National Federation of ASA

Sister Mary Isnard practicing the sacred art of hitting a softball, as she warms up for a season as coach at CYO vacation centers. Many church teams have joined the ASA and other softball associations.

umpires (with more than 34,000 members), the National ASA Scorekeepers Association, and the National Association of Softball Writers & Broadcasters—which has the avowed purpose of getting the media people to wake up and cover the nation's number-one team-participation sport.

Every four years, the ASA sends men's and women's teams to the World Championship of Fast Pitch sponsored by the International Softball Federation. (The U.S. won the 1974 Women's World Championship in Stratford, Connecticut, and the 1976 Men's World Championship in New Zealand.)

Any afficionado of softball is familiar with the ASA Official Guide and Rule Book, an annual publication that contains the ASA code, rules of play, a list of winning teams, most valuable players (MVP's), and pertinent statistics from the previous year's national championships. (Avid collectors keep back issues in locked closets, and the few *complete* collections of ASA guides in existence are guarded by watch dogs. With raised hackles.)

In addition, ASA has a monthly newspaper, *Balls and Strikes,* mailed to every state and 117 foreign countries, with a circulation near 150,000.

Throughout its history, the ASA has maintained its status as a nonprofit and, most emphatically, *amateur* softball organization. Teams are not allowed to make a profit from gate receipts or concessions, and no prize money is awarded for national championships. Though the burden of financial responsibility falls heavily on the sponsors, they must keep smiling and not complain, nor may they recoup their losses through the team's activities. Companies may write it off to advertising, charity, or public relations, but the team itself must remain firmly amateur. (It should be noted that the company's investment may be quite sizable—running as high as thirty to forty thousand dollars for a team that frequents the national tournaments. That includes room, board, traveling expenses, uniforms, and all the rest of it.) Any player who goes professional is immediately disqualified, and he must return to the noble confines of amateurism for one year before being reinstated. In addition, the player is not allowed to compete *against* a professional team, even if he himself does not accept money for the game.

For many years, the limitations of the ASA code meant that ASA teams could only play *other* ASA teams. They were not allowed to play exhibition or charity games where money was taken in at the gate, and they could not accept travel money from outside sources. However, the best players (hotshots or ringers, as they're familiarly called) often move from Company Number One to Company Number Two at a considerable increase in salary and fringe benefits. By offering players good jobs with reasonable hours and a comfortable place to live, the top sponsors have managed to draw players from all around the country. This sort of thing is impossible for the ASA to control.

The other thing ASA doesn't mind is discreet promotion by distributors and manufacturers of softball equipment. Part of getting the rules standardized included getting the cooperation of equipment manufacturers. When the manufacturers of balls, bats, and gloves are meeting criteria, ASA is glad to give its stamp of approval. A number of team managers and owners get into the sporting goods business, but it's all for the good of softball, so no one complains.

Though the ASA is universally recognized as the granddaddy of all softball organizations, there are a number of offspring with strong softball leagues.

The International Softball Congress, a men's fast-pitch amateur league, has a large following in the West, and holds its own tournaments every year. This hybrid organization was founded in 1947 by Larry Walker of Phoenix, Arizona. He had a women's team called Farm Fresh Markets that he named as world champions, and he called his new league the National Softball Congress. His chief rival was Carrol Forbes, an ASA commissioner, who owned a small tire shop in Greeley, Colorado, and sponsored his own team. Forbes challenged the NSC to a softball duel in Oklahoma City, and Walker rose to the occasion. After the tournament, Forbes decided to join the NSC.

During the next two years, the National Softball Congress held its tournaments at Forbes Field in Greeley ("the finest little park in the West"), but in 1950 there came a split between the women's and the men's teams. Larry Walker wanted the NSC to continue promoting women's leagues, but Carrol Forbes thought it should be all-men's fast pitch. They compromised by splitting up. Forbes created the International Softball League, and for seven years the ISL and the

NSC each held their own world tournaments, outside the auspices of the ASA. The top team in the ISL, the Long Beach Nitehawks, won the tournament six years in a row (1955–60), and many softball fans thought the team would beat the Clearwater Bombers, who were the outstanding ASA champs. We'll never know because the ASA would not allow the match to take place. Twenty years later the fans were still asking themselves the big question: Who would have won?

In 1958 the National Softball Congress folded, and Carrol Forbes incorporated its teams into a new, improved International Softball Congress, with headquarters still resting near "the finest little park in the West." In the 1976 tournament there were twenty-six teams on hand for the ten-day extravaganza which was won again by the Long Beach Nitehawks—for the tenth time. But, the long-awaited match between the ISC and the ASA fast-pitch men's teams has yet to take place.

In the slow-pitch department, a major rival with the ASA is the United States Slo-Pitch Softball Association. It was started in 1967 by Ray C. Ernst after a tournament in Louisville, Kentucky, and its headquarters is now in Petersburg, Virginia. The USSSA was a response to the increased popularity of slow-pitch softball, and by 1976 the organization embraced 4,000 teams in a number of different divisions for men and women, including industrial and church leagues. With a structure similar to that of the ASA, the USSSA holds sixteen regional tournaments annually, with world championships in each division.

Until recently, ASA slow-pitch teams were not allowed to play against USSSA teams, even though both were amateur organizations. In some cities, like Baltimore, where the head of the Department of Parks and Rec-reation was an ASA official, this ruling had serious consequences—it meant USSSA teams frequently didn't get permission to play on the metropolitan diamonds. It also meant an ASA team could be disbarred from any tournament for the offense of playing against a USSSA team. In 1975 the USSSA started an anti-trust suit against the ASA, which was settled out of court.

The decision had far-reaching consequences for dedicated members of the softball organizations—and for the ASA especially. According to the terms of the settlement, any USSSA team may compete against an ASA team by becoming a member of that organization—and vice versa. Furthermore, no ASA team may be penalized for playing in a USSSA tournament.

USSSA president, Al Ramsey, was elated by the decision, and for some players it meant the end to long inter-organizational struggles. The attorney from Waynesboro, Virginia, who worked on the case for three years, Larry Palmer, received a plaque from the executive board of the ASA and was given the honor of throwing out the first ball in the 1976 World Series. Three years before, he hadn't known there *was* such a thing as organized softball.

Well, organizations come and go, but there seems to be a special sort of cramp, or crimp, that occasionally comes to the lives of dedicated softballers. It's called SOFA—Softball Organization Friction Addiction. Roughly defined, it's the ability to take all the joy out of softball by spending hours in organizational meetings and conferences, ironing out intra- and inter-organizational difficulties. Perhaps it's a necessary evil—a natural consequence of being too big. But those who love the game stay on the field—they stay away from the SOFA.

TO GO PRO OR NOT TO GO PRO

That is the question. And it's been the question ever since amateur softball got started. At various times thoughout history there have been women's pro teams; in the 1930s Chicago boasted two separate professional women's softball leagues. Attempts have been made to start men's pro fast-pitch leagues, with the idea that it's just as much fun to watch as pro baseball. There have also been a number of exhibition teams—some only four players—that travel the country challenging the best (non-ASA) competitors in each area. And every now and then a hotshot team will pull up its amateur roots and go barnstorming for a month or a season, just to prove that people can make money even if they have fun doing it.

The years 1976 and 1977 saw the founding of two ambitious professional leagues—the International Women's Professional Softball Association and (for men) the American Professional Slo-Pitch League.

The women's league plays fast pitch and includes star players who have been recruited from the top amateur women's teams all across the country. From the very beginning, all eyes were on Joan Joyce—a former player for the Raybestos Brakettes (Stratford, Connecticut)—who started the league along with Billie Jean King, the tennis star, and Jane Blalock, the golf pro. They had the financial backing of Dennis Murphy, a founder of the American Basketball Association, World Hockey Association, and World Team Tennis. In the first season, 1976, there were ten teams, and Joan Joyce's Falcons (Eastern Division) won the first World Series against the San Jose Sunbirds (Western Division).

WPS went into the 1977 season with fewer teams—eight instead of ten—a longer pitching distance and a new public relations firm. The Falcons and Sunbirds were back, and California contributed two new teams—the Bakersfield Aggie's and the Santa Ana Lionettes. With each team scheduled for eighty-four games, the top four teams would go into the play-offs. In the new WPS rules, the pitching mound was moved from the previous year's distance of 40 feet to a longer distance of 44, in hopes that the game would produce more hitting—to make it more exciting for spectators.

Contracts for players ranged from about $1,000 to $3,000 for the season, and some players complained that they had to wash their own uniforms and pay for other small expenses. Many of the women players were athletic coaches or gym instructors who would return to their teaching jobs in the fall. As pros, the players had the benefit of top competition throughout the season, but some of them missed the camaraderie they'd enjoyed as free-wheeling amateurs. As one pitcher complained to a reporter, "I can see I'm going to

A professional pitcher for Parichy Bloomer Girls of Chicago in 1941, Dorothy "Boots" Klupping Ortman earned $95 pitching one night a week. Off-season, she was a fourth-grade teacher at Maywood Grade School.

Bert Smith, home-run hitter for the Detroit Caesars in the American Professional Slo-Pitch League. In the first weekend of professional play, Smith hit 6 home runs in 11 times at bat.

have to change my style. I'll have to treat it like a job."

On the men's side of the park, the spectators were asked to pay to watch slow pitch—a very different game, where the pitching is hardly worth mentioning, home runs are frequent, and top-notch fielding is essential. The American Pro Slo-Pitch League was officially launched in 1977, with Bill Byrne as its founder, and former baseball star Whitey Ford as League Commissioner. Franchises were sold in twelve cities for $25,000 each, with additional team funds in escrow for tournaments, travel, and expenses. In its first year the APSPL consisted of the Baltimore Monuments, Pittsburgh Hardhats, New Jersey Statesmen, New York Clippers, Cleveland Jaybirds, Columbus All-Americans, Cincinnati Suds (slogan: "Suds in your beer, suds in your washer, and now suds go pro."), Kentucky Bourbons, Chicago Storm, Detroit Caesars, Milwaukee Copper Hearth, and Minnesota Goofy's.

Recruitment was so fast and furious at the beginning of the 1977 season that it became a joke among the amateurs. One manager of a slow-pitch team noticed one of his players standing by the telephone in the dugout. "What're you doing over there?" asked the manager. "Just waiting for that phone call," said the player.

But it wasn't so funny when those 6′3″, 210-pound sluggers began missing amateur practice, and finally phoned in the news that they'd "gone pro." Salaries, for the most part, are small—in the $1,000 to $5,000 range—and a few players were going to $1.00 a game just to play against the top competition. But there was no doubt about it—pro ball left many gaps in the amateur teams in its first season. None of the players were giving up their jobs yet, and the double-headers were all played on weekends. But there was a $100,000 kitty guaranteed to the four teams that made the play-offs—$50,000 to the winner, $25,000 for second place, with $15,000 to third and $10,000 to fourth.

At the World Series in September, 1977, Detroit Caesars took the championship in four straight games against the Baltimore Monuments, with the Kentucky Bourbons and Cleveland Jaybirds in third and fourth place. Season attendance averaged 2,818 at each game in the League, and more than 10,000 showed up for the World Series games in Detroit and Baltimore.

In Cleveland, always a hot spot for softball, I attended the opening game in May between the Cleveland Jaybirds and the New Jersey Statesmen. Fans numbering 6,542 crowded into Rose Field at Brookside Park to watch the best Cleveland players knock out the New Jersey Statesmen, 22–12 and 9–2. On a steep cliffside behind the ball park, more spectators sat and stood around the ledge, watching the game for free from a 60-foot aerie. Jay Friedman and Don Rardin, co-owners of the Jaybirds, came onto the field before the game and said how pleased they were to see everybody. A 68-year-old toothless concessionaire wearing a paper "Stroh's Beer" cap walked up and down in front of the bleachers getting applause for his beer-drinking feats. He sold some, too. The right fielder for the Statesmen was booed off the field after missing two fly balls. John Spadaccino, better known as the "Italian Stallion," wasn't doing much for the Statesmen either. But the Jaybirds had Dave Jakubs, Rich Petrunyak, and Jim Vaccarina on their side, and together they weighed about 600 pounds, and when they hit the Dudley Nite-Ball, it didn't come back. It just disappeared over the fence, and sometimes over the stands, where the kids fought for it while the citizens of Cleveland got hoarse yelling for their favorites. Between innings, a spectator could overhear the folks in the bleachers talking about what Dave was like in high school, or what Steve Loya (6′2″, 230 lbs.) batted when he played for Pyramid Cafe, and how Richie's mother was so proud of him she sat right behind him in the outfield, with all of his friends around—just listen to them yell!

Pro or not, it's still softball, and softball doesn't belong to the franchise. It belongs to us.

At least that's what they say in Cleveland.

Chapter 2

HOTSHOTS, REGULARS, AND GOOD-TIMERS

HOTSHOTS

The real hotshot has no trouble finding a sponsor—sports store, beer company, brake-lining manufacturer, or local Chevy dealer. Hotshots belong to the best teams in the country, teams that go into the national tournaments decked out in the finest uniforms, with all the trappings of major league ballplayers. They have first-class managers, a competent batboy and a scorekeeper who knows the difference between a hit and an error. They play on ball fields that are groomed to perfection. The base lines are marked out in white chalk. The infield is raked between games. Home plate is brushed off by a conscientious umpire who, incidentally, got a 20-20 at his last eye examination. The games are properly officiated, coached, and managed, and the outcomes reported to all the correct authorities. Hotshots play by the book.

Of course, there are many hotshots in fast pitch—clustered around those extraordinary pitchers who make teams famous—as well as in the slow-pitch game. But today most hotshot players are gravitating to slow-pitch squads where fielding is fast and hitting is fierce. One such team is Pepsico of Long Island, managed by George "Doc" Linnehan.

Doc, a former chiropractor and owner of County Sports in Levittown, New York, is an inveterate softball player who has managed teams for almost thirty years. From 1956 to 1966 his teams played championship fast pitch in the Eastern Seaboard Major Softball League (which he served as president). Unlike some managers who resisted the emigration from fast pitch to slow, Doc saw the way the ball was rolling, and in 1966 he started an all-new slow-pitch team, which he managed along with a former Yankee star southpaw, Marius Russo. That team went to the nationals the first year, and in 1968 (with Doc as sole manager), it won the ASA National Men's Major Slow-Pitch Championship at Jones Beach, taking seven out of eight games in the tournament. Between 1968 and 1976, though Doc's teams didn't win the championship again, they never lost a single game in the regional competition and they compiled a record 55 wins against 23 defeats in national ASA competition. As team expenses rose beyond the means of the modest County Sports store, Doc sought the support of the Empire Vending Company, which was co-sponsor for a couple of years. In 1976 Pepsico became the sole sponsor of Doc's team. (The large corporation, which has a concentrate division in Queens, spent nearly $25,000 that year fully subsidizing everything from cost of uniforms to room and board at tournaments.) The team name was changed appropriately from County Sports to Empire Vending-County Sports and finally to Pepsico. In 1977 Doc was elected to the ASA Hall of Honor as one of the outstanding managers in the nation, and in June of the same year he conducted softball clinics in Helsinki, Moscow, and Oslo as part of a cultural exchange program sponsored by the U. S. State Department.

The man behind the reputation is in his sixties, with graying hair and a way of moving that almost looks like a shuffle—but isn't. His County Sports shop specializes in softball equipment, naturally, and every spring it turns into a glorified warehouse operation as orders for uniforms, hats, shoes, balls, bats, and gloves pour over the counter. As representative for the Dudley Sports Company in the Northeast, Doc has to keep the greater New England area fully stocked with softball miscellany, including hundreds of dozens of the Dudley balls. (Hotshots, of course, always buy their softballs by the dozen.) Wearing a loose cardigan, sitting in a one-arm swivel chair in front of a battered oak desk, surrounded by files and boxes of clippings and

calendars of forthcoming games and tournaments, Doc manages the store and plots his strategy for the season.

On the ball field, he's a different person. He taps fungoes to the outfielders with a steady, persistent plonk-plonk-plonk, swinging the aluminum bat in a manner that can only be described as casual. He frames his orders in the form of quiet suggestions. He coaches third base with the detachment of a traffic warden watching a bad traffic snarl from a helicopter. It's not exactly your image of a tough-talking, two-fisted, fire-breathing manager, but Doc's method seems to get the job done. Besides, he's got a veteran team that doesn't need to be kicked, and those who have played for him say he *can* be stubborn as a mule.

Doc is as proud of the character-rating of his hotshots as he is of their averages. One of the most famous players for County-Sports-turned-Pepsico was Jimmy Galloway, better known to thousands of fans as "Mr. Softball." He played on Doc's teams from 1966 to 1976, but in 1977—much to Doc's regret—Galloway "went pro" and joined the New York Clippers in the American Pro Slo-Pitch League.

In the softball world, Galloway has been called "a legend in his own time." Standing 6′4″, weighing 235 pounds, he has a tendency to smash the ball so hard it frequently travels several hundred feet and leaps an improbable distance beyond the fence. (Typical brutal performance: At the 1972 Rheingold Softball Tournament of Champions, Galloway hit 11 home runs in 23 times at bat.) Everywhere the team travels, children crowd around "Mr. Softball" to get his autograph, and the fans in Parma, Springfield, Maryville, and Pittsburgh throng to the park to see Jimmy Galloway in action.

Another star of the Pepsico squad is the team's home-run-artist and pinch hitter, Oscar

Jimmy Galloway at bat for County Sports of Long Island. As an amateur, Galloway was elected to the All-American slow-pitch team a record eight times.

Steadman. Oscar, who was called "one of the best all-round athletes to come out of Glen Cove High School," has put on a bit of weight since high school days, and his knees are bad, so he runs with approximately the velocity of a skateboarder going uphill. But can he hit! Not only that, he has faithfully served the team as batting coach, resident wit, temperamental slugger, Jimmy Galloway supporter, and all-round wise guy. Short, black, and round-bellied, he comes to spring practice with a multicolored porkpie hat squashed on his head, and he sprinkles the field with a variety of hits that are called up at will.

During the week, Oscar drives a wholesale produce truck in the mornings, and coaches at a youth recreation center in the afternoons. As a "market man," he has to get to the Clinton Market in the Bronx at 2 A.M., where he waits for the fruit and vegetables to come in, then loads up and makes deliveries. Occasionally he's too tired to play softball in the evening, but he makes it to most of the games. His philosophy is simple:

"I think everyone in the world should play softball," he says. "That would solve all the world's problems."

Be that as it may, Doc Linnehan and Oscar have had their moments. At one tournament Oscar sat on the bench through every single game without a single turn at bat. He was furious and wouldn't speak to Doc all the following week. But the next weekend, with no explanation, Doc put Oscar in right field so he would be in the regular line-up. Still seething, the slugger took out his aggression on the 12-inch ball, and hit a home run every time a pitch came his way. After the game, Doc went up to him and said with a sigh, "Oscar, I guess I just gotta keep you mad all the time. It's the only way you'll keep hittin'!"

Like any hotshot team, the Pepsico players have a host of memories of hard-fought tournaments, tough teams, and outstanding players.

Nearly all softball tournaments are double elimination. A team that loses in the first or second round of play is automatically bumped into the "losers' bracket," where it gets a second chance to fight its way to the top. The logistics of this kind of tournament are complicated, but the purpose is to give every team a second chance. If it fights its way through the losers' bracket, the team will meet the champion from the "winners' bracket" in the final games. But there's one big difference: in the winners' bracket, the top team only runs through a total of six or seven games to win. In the losers' bracket, the team might have to go through ten or eleven rounds in making a comeback. A reasonably fresh and well-rested team from the winners' bracket has an obvious advantage over the losers' squad, which has had to claw, hack, and swat its way up from

the bottom of the heap. The charm of the final games is that there is an obviously exhausted, haggard, fierce underdog—the guys from the losers' bracket—fighting against a self-satisfied bully from the winners'. Obviously, anyone with a decent sense of justice will be cheering for the underdog.

In 1966 Pepsico almost got out of just such a pickle—and it's a tournament that none of the players will ever forget. Nor will the couple thousand folks from Parma, Ohio, who stayed up all of a drizzly Sunday night to see it to the bitter end.

It was the team's first year in slow pitch, and Doc had the misfortune in the opening game to draw Skip Hogan's A.C., the championship team from the previous year. A.C. had a rude and clownish pitcher named Louis Delmastro, a man known for his exuberant stunts and acerbic remarks, and County Sports lost the opener, 13–5. That was on Friday night, and the defeat sent the Long Island team straight to the depths of the losers' bracket. On Saturday the rain gods took over the field, with thunder, bolts of lightning, and floods of water until twelve noon on Sunday. That moisture set back the whole tournament schedule, and as the boys scrambled out on the muddy field, they knew they had a long ordeal ahead of them.

County Sports started to win. It beat Wisconsin, 11–6; walloped Illinois, 20–8; smashed Minneapolis, 20–11; slid by Connecticut, 10–9; trounced Stotz of New York, 18–8; humiliated Indiana, 16–11; struck Helf-Erie Sheet Steel of Cleveland with a 7–3 hammer blow; brazened its way past Milwaukee, 20–14; rode roughshod over Wilsman Trucking of Ohio, 25–9; and insulted the host team of Swing Inn, Cleveland, by swinging them off the field with an 18–17 victory. With all this walloping, smashing, and trouncing, plus the mud on the playing field and the humidity in the air, the County Sports boys were well-nigh exhausted by the time they faced the winners'

The hotshots of Empire-County Sports, 1975. Top row, l. to r.: Bill Molloy, L. Russo, S. Shurina, L. Chiappetta, M. Foley, J. Konicki, O. Steadman, W. Williams. Middle row: Timmy Williams, batboy; Doc Linnehan, manager; J. Davidi, E. Finnegan (?), George Linnehan. Front row: Bob Rolleich, C. Menzel, B. Shugman, G. Richter, S. Becalorri, J. Galloway.

champs, Michael's Lounge from Detroit, Michigan. It was the hour of judgment—more precisely, it was 5 A.M. Monday morning.

Detroit got 14 hits to the Long Islanders' 3, winning the final match by a score of 10–0. The last game ended at 7 A.M. Monday morning.

Before the ordeal was over, most of the County Sports team had less than five hours' sleep in forty-eight hours, and the players were on the field a total of thirty-one hours. Attendance at Parma stadium topped 25,000, and many of the faithful stayed in the

bleachers throughout Sunday night, seeing County Sports win game after game—only to lose in the last.

During the 10-game winning streak, Long Island recorded 41 home runs. Jimmy Galloway accounted for 11 of those, and Bill Brown—whom one sportswriter called "the best pitcher in the country"—collected 7. A baseball and football coach from Roosevelt High in New York, Len Mackalavage had 4 home runs, including a grand slam, and a total of 17 RBI's in the tournament.

It was not until two years later that the

underdog got the National Championship. In 1968 County Sports won the National in a final-round double-header against Jo's House of Pizza from Milton, Florida. The scores in the last two games were 11–7 and 17–12.

For Pepsico and other hotshot slow-pitch teams, the home run is an essential item. Eight or nine men in every line-up must have home-run potential if the team is to blaze a trail to the national championship. They must have the height, bulk, and raw muscle required to send a ball more than three hundred feet through the air, and they must also have the fielding ability required to snag powerfully hit grounders and line drives.

Some home-run hitters are born. It is clear in the maternity ward that they will weigh 223 pounds, measure 6'3", have shoulders like Hercules and forearms the size of your average telephone pole. It isn't long before a manager from one of the nation's slow-pitch team arrives at the door, offering to buy the youngster a new glove and take him to dinner.

The next thing you know, the hotshot is going to all the tournaments and hitting home runs. There's something intimidating about his profound silence as he steps toward the warm-up box, drawing a batting glove on over his thick paw. He picks up a metal bat, slides a weighted "doughnut" over the handle down to the shaft, and tries a few practice swings. He leads from the shoulder, not too fast and not too slow, like a butcher wielding a meat ax. Then he steps up to home plate.

The catcher, huddled in the box, looks hard at the pitcher, and flashes a signal. The pitcher looks hard at the catcher and scuffles his feet in the dust. The ump rests his hands on his knees, measures the space between the batter's knees and his shoulders with a practiced eye. All three—pitcher, catcher, umpire—act as if they're trying to forget the exist-ence of the batter. It's like trying to wish Goliath off the face of the earth.

He won't go away. Immense, tyrannical, poised for the kill, this mountain of muscle hangs over the plate. It's an awesome sight.

The pitcher balances on the mound. With a swift arm motion that seems almost to express desperation, he hurls a slow, deceptive pitch that falls in close to the plate.

"Striiiiike one," calls the ump, holding up his left hand.

The batter glances over his shoulder. Strike? he seems to say. Strike, ump? You call that a strike? Huh? The ump tries, harder than ever, not to look at this big guy.

The next two are balls. Then another strike. Two and two. The teams don't speak. The crowd doesn't murmur. The batter looks—well, sort of deadly. Something's gonna happen.

Something does happen.

The next pitch comes across as a medium arc, with a touch of speed. A sort of electricity runs through the all-powerful human frame from head to toe. The arms drag backward, lifting the bat—the Neanderthal's club—higher in the air. The ball is in there. Then it isn't.

There is the PLONK of a metal bat connecting with a leather ball, and suddenly no one is looking at the batter any more. Every heart and every eye follow a white orb that grows smaller as it rises higher and—supported by the force of human will, driven on the whiplash of human aggression—soars out beyond the farthest outfielder and drops over the fence.

The rest is ritual. The slow, loping run around the bases. The team's rush out of the bullpen to shake the hand of the crusher that did the deed. The haughty insouciance, the trace of a smile as the hotshot accepts the backwhacks and rear slaps and handshakes. Chalk up one more.

In the upper echelons of the slow-pitch kingdom, the games are dominated by these kinds of mammoth hitters. Teams like Pepsico, Warren Motors, Howard's Furniture, Jerry's Catering, Bunch Brothers, and Duggan & Duggan have dozens of immense players who have fallen into the habit of bashing the ball an unbelievable distance nearly every time they step up to the plate.

They are not to be blamed personally for such brutality—they can't help themselves. That's just the way it is among hotshots.

REGULARS

You can see them coming a mile away. They're wearing cut-off jeans and T-shirts, carrying worn-out shoes with spikes, and played-out gloves that look like they've been through the swamp a few times. They chew gum, smoke cigarettes, carry bags and sacks and backpacks stuffed with beer and sandwiches and junk food. They call themselves the Regulars.

The Regulars are a loosely organized group of New Yorkers who play softball every Saturday morning in Central Park. Since 1969 the self-appointed Regulars have been meeting weekly on the corner diamond across from the Delacorte Theater (where "Shakespeare in the Park" is presented). They come in all ages—from 23 to 52, but the median is about 30—and from a wide range of professional backgrounds. They usually play three or four games during the day—quitting in early afternoon—and their teams are selected according to a unique choose-up system.

Remember how we used to pick teams in the old days? You had two captains, Jesse and Chris. Jesse chose "odds" and Chris chose "evens." They faced each other, making fists with their right hands, and said, "One, two, three, shoot." On the word "shoot," they stuck out one, two, or three fingers. If the total number of fingers was odd, then Jesse got first choice. (He always chose Ron because Ron was the best hitter. He sure didn't choose me; I could hardly get a dink single through the infield.) Anyway, that was the way they did it in *my* neighborhood.

But the Regulars don't do it that way. The rule among them is that the first twenty Regulars to arrive in the morning make up the first two teams. They play one game, and the winning team stays on the field. Then a new, challenging team is made up of the guys who haven't played yet, plus *some* of the Regulars from the first team. The question is, how do you become a Regular in the first place? Ah, there's the rub . . .

The selection, in fact, is done by a careful process of discussion and diplomacy. Rule of thumb is: once a Regular, always a Regular. You can't be fired, even if your knees start to wobble and your hair turns gray. But it's damn tough to become a permanent Regular. The guys that want to be Regulars show up one Saturday after another, with glove and beer and togs, all set to play. They don't get

The Regulars, pursuing a rigorous schedule of calisthenics between games in Central Park. How many dogs can you find in this picture? How many softball players?

on a team automatically, however. The already-accepted Regulars get first preference, and it's highly unlikely that a new man will have a chance to join in the first game, or even the second game, unless he has a very strong lobby working for him. By the third game, however, some of the Regulars are tired or have headaches or are feeling mellow after a few beers, so they drop out giving the new guys a chance.

The new guy can help his cause by showing initiative and ambition—but without being too pushy. If he turns up week after week, his determination will probably be noted and eventually rewarded. If he shows a willingness to serve as umpire, coach third

base, or do some fielding practice between games, the Regulars will begin calling him "okay." And once you're "okay," you're almost "in." Persistence will pay off.

The Regulars generally prefer an umpire selected from among themselves. That gives the new guys a chance to get in the thick of the game, and it also saves the cost of hiring a professional umpire. Once in a while, though, the Regulars call on "Sid" to be their ump.

Now, Sid is a crusty, knobby-kneed veteran of the umping world who is extremely prone to asserting his authority. Sid wears navy blue Bermuda shorts—which, as far as I know, is unique attire for an ump. He uses a genuine horsehair paintbrush instead of a

Sid Bronsky, the Regular's formidable ump, calls two strikes loud and clear. Let no man say nay.

whisk broom to sweep off home plate. When Sid calls an out, he punches the air with his hairy right fist, and the bellow that comes from his lungs sounds like a diesel engine starting up.

The trouble with Sid is this authority thing. Sid is extremely vehement about calling ball and strike, safe and out, right and wrong. And sometimes the Regulars don't go for this arbiter of justice, not at all. One example, drawn from a sunny forenoon in July, will show you why:

It's the top of the seventh inning, and the team at bat is behind by 2. There's one out, with the bases loaded. Next man up hits an infield grounder, and the shortstop throws to second for a force out. The second baseman has to avoid the runner to make the throw to first—but he doesn't get it off in time, and the runner is safe at first. One out, right?

Nope. Sid calls *two* outs. One for the force out and one for the runner interfering with the second baseman. H-m-m. That makes three outs, and the end of the game.

The Regulars are incredulous. At first they are merely speechless, but gradually the losing team gets wound up for a big argument. Hands are waved in Sid's face. Sid's calm explanation turns into a roar. Jaws flap. Threats are made.

One of the Regulars who works weekdays as a psychiatrist steps into the fray, and gradually things calm down. Sid even gets paid. But still there are grumblings. Never again, say the Regulars, will we have Sid.

Sid grins, two teeth missing. "I call them as I see them," he says.

At the end of the season, the Regulars get together and have a huge awards banquet where everyone behaves atrociously and awards are handed out for individual records, highest averages, and MVP's. (There's a score-keeper at every game, and the Regulars check up on him frequently to make sure they haven't been wrongly accused of making an error.) The Regular's yearbook, containing all the records, is passed hand-to-hand around the table. During the banquet, one member of the Regulars reads a speech that is loaded with off-color references, and sometimes the management of the restaurant offers to send them all home because of their unruly behavior. But the Regulars aren't really unruly—they're just exuberant softballers—and the year-end celebration is the high point of the season. Or, if you look at it the other way, the promise of another, better season to come.

Neil Jenney, a Soho artist, travels uptown to play catcher for the Regulars every weekend. He owns nine pairs of gray-flannel baseball trousers and an unknown number of suspenders.

GOOD-TIMERS

They arrive, incognito, at Sunday picnics, family reunions, camping expeditions, block parties, alumni get-togethers, and Memorial Day weekends. They can be friends, aunts, uncles, cousins, sisters, brothers, fathers, mothers, with maybe a generation before and a generation after thrown in, all headed for the same piece of grass. Slightly sweaty, impatient with the week gone by, but generally in good spirits. Their clothing is sparse and colorful, their air flamboyant. Watching them invade the park, school ground, or lawn, you'd hardly suspect what they were up to. You'd think: maybe a picnic, maybe a game of Frisbee. That's what you'd guess, judging from their disguises.

You'd be wrong. They're here to play softball. Once you know that, you begin to notice details. The glove under Freddy's arm. The bat protruding from a shoulder bag. The softball clenched between the teeth of the family dog.

Good-timers of all ages are the real heart and soul of softball. They play because . . . well, who knows why they play? Because somebody brought along a bat and ball, that's why. Because Freddy is gonna nag his dad and mom and sister and everybody else until *someone* throws the ball to him. They'll play because Ann wants to hit that thing, and Dad wants to catch it. Because the sun is shining, and they've got lots of food in the basket, and because they're friends or family, and because

. . . well, because it's wonderful to play softball.

"C'mon, throw it," says Freddy.

"Wait, we gotta have bases," says Ann.

"Here are some napkins. Dottie, we're gonna use these napkins," says Dad.

"For *bases?* Frank, are you out of your mind? Those are our best napkins!" says Mom.

"Wait, I've got a rock," says Ann.

"Not a rock, stupid," says Freddy. "You want someone to break his ankle."

"I won't break *my* ankle."

"You can't use rocks as bases."

"You can too."

"Can not."

"Can too."

"Will you kids cut that out! You're gettin' on my nerves."

"Daddy, Ann says we should use *rocks!*"

"I know, I know, I heard the whole . . ."

"I can't believe it. Girls are so stupid."

"Well, you think of something better."

"Here's a piece of cardboard."

"That's fine. Can we get four bases out of it?"

"I think so . . ." (*rrrriiipppp*) "Woops."

"Ah, now look what you did."

Well, the bases may be cardboard, and the base lines won't be quite accurate, and third may be a little closer to home plate than first, but when good-timers play, the technicalities aren't important. You just take what you have and make a game. If your field is only as wide as a city street, then that's as good as Yankee Stadium. Put your bases on the curb and play. If there are trees in right field, just call it a double every time the ball goes in the trees. If you only have six players, the team at bat has to supply a catcher for the team that's pitching, and he has to play like he's on their side. If there are only five players on a side, you aren't allowed more than a double on an outfield hit. With four players, use one base and make "fair" territory a narrow alley. With three players, try flies-and-grounders or one-o'cat. If it's just you and the other guy, play catch or have him hit some fungoes. If you're all alone, toss some fly balls

in the air and catch them. Someone will join you soon. People can't resist.

All good-timers will understand that they have to make up some unorthodox rules so everyone can have a good time. Among these:

1. A player may join or leave a game at any time, for any reason, unless his teammates holler violent objections. Valid reasons for leaving the game are: (a) Need to go to the bathroom, (b) bored, (c) object to the attitudes of the other players, (d) not having a good time. If teammates do holler violent objections, then you'll have to make up your mind whether you're going to be decent and stay in the game, or just walk away like a selfish so-and-so who doesn't give a *hoot* for your team. Boy, you better *not* walk out on them.

2. The game is over when everyone's hungry and/or tired.

3. The people at the next picnic table can join if they want to, but they have to keep their dog away from first base.

4. Freddy gets as many strikes as he wants because he's only six years old.

5. Ann also gets unlimited strikes, even though she's eight. That's because she insists on it.

6. Bases can be moved only before or after a play. None of that stuff where the first baseman picks it up and runs for right field. Like you tried last time.

7. Grandpa can get someone to run for him.

8. Grandma has to run for herself.

9. Whoever plays first base gets to use the biggest glove.

Rule Number 10: Good-Timers, especially young ones, are allowed to swing anyway they like. Note spread-handed grip, unorthodox stance, and superb concentration.

Among good-timers there are occasional disputes about who is making concessions to whom. If Ann feels that her father is giving her easier pitches than Freddy, she has a perfect right to feel outraged. She knows she can hit better than Freddy, so why shouldn't she get the same pitches? Ann, in this case, is perfectly right and her father is dead wrong. He's living in the dark ages when people believed you had to pitch easier to girls and all that bologna. There's a good chance Ann will be hitting a lot better than her father in a couple of years, so he'd better pitch right.

On the other hand, some concessions must be made. If you're the mother of these children, and you've had a terrible week with them, take out your aggressions on the ball, but not on the kids. Go ahead and hit a line drive, but please don't hit it *directly* at your son the pitcher. (Or, if you must, say to him: "Freddy, this is going to be a hard line drive down the middle, 'cause you really got on my nerves this week, so you better duck.")

Young people must also make concessions to their parents on the playing field. They should not mimic their overweight father, no matter how silly he looks running to first base. (Or, as Freddy says, "You call that running?") They should not call Aunt Hilda a "nut" just because she swings the bat like a wild lady. They should not laugh at their grandmother when she slides into third base. More kids these days need to be taught to respect their elders, or at least not make fun of them right in front of their faces.

The main thing that good-timers have to watch out for is the habitual show-off. He or she may be a member of the family or group, or might suddenly ask to join in just for the purpose of showing off. At first, you might not notice what this person is doing, but after a while you realize that this person is not really playing with you. This person is looking out for himself, apparently to prove something. This person will throw the ball very hard to someone who isn't wearing a glove. This person will step right over Freddy in order to catch a fly ball. When Freddy says, "That was mine," this person will say, "Oh, you never woulda caught that one." This person is so objectionable I won't even tell you this person's name.

You have to watch out because a show-off can ruin a good-timer's game. A show-off gets impatient with everyone else because he thinks they're beneath him, and eventually a show-off can get people hurt by throwing too hard or sliding into bases or grabbing all the fly balls. When anyone gets hurt in a good-timer game, every one goes away feeling just miserable. Good-timers play for fun, not for keeps, and they like to leave the field in a better mood than when they came on. Real good-timers always feel like leaving the field together in a bunch.

The sun is setting, the air is getting cool, and you can still smell the smoke from those hotdogs and hamburgs that have been getting overcooked on the grill that day. The picnic basket is lighter. Everybody's feeling a bit sleepy, and Freddy just lets the bag drag through the grass as they cross the field. It seems to take forever to get where they're going. But who cares? It was a great day for softball, and home isn't far away.

Chapter 3

UNDERHAND COMBAT

TURF AND STUFF

The Field. There are softball diamonds all over the place, but the problem is that the sport is growing faster than the land mass allotted to it. Which means you've got to get your application in early if you want to play, say, every Thursday night at six o'clock on a lighted field. In most urban areas the fields are assigned in early spring by the Department of Parks and Recreation, but in small towns the fields are often run by the Elks, VFW, or the high school's department of recreation, and these organizations give club or school teams first preference. Sometimes there's some funny business when it comes to handing out permits. In New York, probably the nation's capital of funny business, a season's permit must be arranged three months in advance.

"We have had many more applicants to use fields than we can possibly cope with," said Martin Lang, head of N.Y.C.'s Department of Parks and Recreation at the beginning of the 1977 season. He added, "It's so bad that I've been getting calls from political figures who try to bring pressure to get permits for teams."

If you don't have a politico on your side, it's nice to have seniority. For instance, teams like Beejays and Dailey's Pub in Queens, which belong to the Glendale Softball Association, have been playing the gin-mill circuit in the Russell Sage Junior High schoolyard in Queens for years and years. Renewal of their permit is almost automatic.

The diagram on the next page shows standard dimensions for a softball diamond—but if you're using a park field, it's probably laid out already. Just make sure you're on a softball diamond, not a baseball diamond: the one you want is the smaller. If your field looks like the town dump, you'll want to hold a "clean-up day" and offer everyone a free beer for every five pounds of garbage raked in. Other things to do (checklist for the organizer):

1. Get an ump. Professional umpires can be recommended by the Department of Recreation or a local softball association. There's a fee, but if everyone chips in fifty cents a game, you've about covered it.

2. Find the bases. Are they in the locker

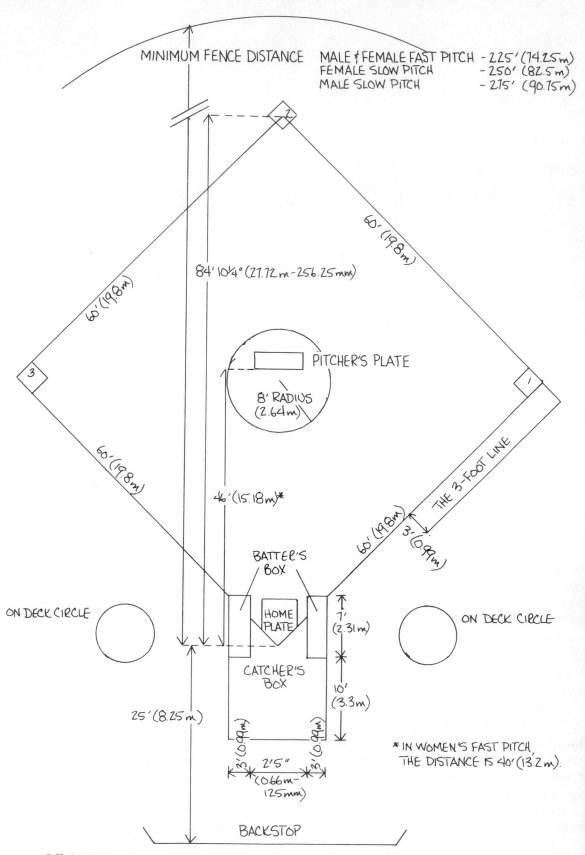

MINIMUM FENCE DISTANCE MALE & FEMALE FAST PITCH - 225' (74.25m)
FEMALE SLOW PITCH   - 250' (82.5m)
MALE SLOW PITCH   - 275' (90.75m)

60' (19.8m)

84' 10¼" (27.72 m - 256.25mm)

PITCHER'S PLATE

8' RADIUS
(2.64m)

THE 3-FOOT LINE

46' (15.18m)*

60' (19.8m)

3' (0.99m)

BATTER'S BOX

ON DECK CIRCLE

HOME PLATE

ON DECK CIRCLE

7' (2.31m)

CATCHER'S BOX

10' (3.3m)

25' (8.25m)

3' (0.99m)

3' (0.99m)

2'5" (0.66m - 125mm)

* IN WOMEN'S FAST PITCH, THE DISTANCE IS 40' (13.2 m).

BACKSTOP

Official Dimensions of Softball Diamonds, as approved by the International Joint Rules Committee on Softball.

room? The recreation office? Under the stands? How come we always gotta go looking for the bases?

3. Specify general rules. You've probably decided in advance whether it's to be slow pitch, fast pitch, or modified, but there are so many variations that it's best to come to some kind of agreement before the game. In slow pitch, especially, you might want to ask the ump what he's going to call a strike. Some umpires want to see a nice high arc. Others will allow a pretty speedy ball, even in slow pitch. As for the fine details, you can't do better than the Official Softball Rules, copyright the International Joint Rules Committee on Softball, and revised yearly. It's available at most sports stores that carry softball equipment, or through organizations like the ASA and USSSA.

4. Clarify special rules. If the ball goes into the oak tree in right field, is it still in play? What happens if a spectator picks up a fair ball? What if it lands on the roof of the hotdog stand? Is the first-baseman's wife allowed to pinch hit? Are we gonna allow stealing? Who calls the game in case it rains? How come I'm the only guy who understands the rules around here?

The ball. The official 12-inch softball actually measures between 11⅞ and 12⅛ inches in circumference, and the best varieties have a leather cover with hand-stitched, flat seams. Some companies make softballs with rubber, Naugahyde, or synthetic covers that are cheaper but perform differently from the leather-covered balls and may turn mushy. No hotshot would deign to play with such an item.

Several softball companies make a "restricted flight" ball that's used by most slow-pitch teams; it flies, all right, but not quite as far as the "unlimited flight" ball. The "unlimited" is used for fast pitch, since really long hits are less common in that game. If you're going to be playing under lights, it's advisable to use a "night ball" with a chalk-white cover —though most softballs are now made with the white cover.

The ASA or USSSA have endorsed certain brands of softball—Dudley, Harwood, Worth, deBeer—but there are other balls available which may be equally reliable. The price, in most cases, is a fair reflection of the quality of the ball, running from about $1.75 to $4.50 retail for a single ball. But balls are most expensive when bought singly, and if your team will be wearing them out all season, it's cheaper to buy them by the dozen.

The Bat. The softball bat is shorter and lighter than a baseball bat, so don't walk into the wrong department at your local sports store. Incidentally, it's perfectly all right to stand there in the aisle gripping the bat firmly and giving it a few slow practice swings. The clerks know softballers have a touch of mania, and they won't come near you. Just watch out for the innocent customer standing behind you.

In any well-stocked store you're going to be faced with an awesome variety of bats, and it's best to do your research in the field, so you know what you want. There are wooden bats made of good old solid oak and metal bats which are aluminum filled with a plastic foam, with rubber-coated handles. Rules allow for plastic and bamboo bats, too.

The wooden bat is cheaper (in the neighborhood of $5.00), but the metal bat (closer to $15) is now being used by most of the hotshots. You have an array of choices in both flavors. There's the Brute, the Countess, the Fireball, the Blue Bomber, the Bombat, the Big Barrell S8, a Big Daddy, Max-Max-Max S8, a Goliath, a Krasher, a Black Tornado, a Black Max S9 "Bottle Bat," a Hot Bat, a Mag Bat, a Superbat, and who hasn't heard of the Louisville Slugger. Of course, you can avoid the whole unbearable dilemma of selecting a bat by joining a team with a good collection and using whatever suits your bicep.

The glove, on the other hand, is one of the most personal items you can own and must be chosen with exquisite care. If you are tempted to buy someone (even a little kid) a glove for birthday or Christmas, here's a word of advice: Don't. Give your softball fanatic a gift certificate, and let him choose his own. It's got to feel right and fit right. He's going to be finicky about the size of the web, the shape of the pocket, and the feel of the leather palm. He'll reject what looks to you like a perfectly serviceable glove, just because it's not "right" for his hand. He'll seize an item that appears big enough to snag basketballs. You don't know what he'll choose, so you shouldn't decide for him. Besides, how do you make up your mind between a Big Daddy tri-action LSC-10 with a ball-trap pocket and stabber web, and a Super Monster M1000 with rawhide lacing, welted seams, all wool-felt palm, and a patented cup-trap pocket? No, better to get a gift certificate and leave the choice up to your softball nut.

Warning: It may have to be a very fat gift certificate. You can still get away with something in the $15 category for a very young kid, but when he gets smarter, he's going to want something in the $25–$30 range. Hotshots, these days, are grabbing gloves that go from $50 to $80 and over, so you see why they need sponsors. Softball gloves and baseball gloves are the same brands, but the softball player goes for the one with a larger "trap" or "web" in the area between thumb and index finger.

The quality of leather is one thing that determines the price of a glove, and the better gloves usually have more handwork in their construction. Since leather lacing is done by hand, the glove with the most lacing is more likely to show qualities of endurance. Catcher and first baseman are permitted to wear mitts

—which usually have more padding in the palm.

Breaking in a glove is a ritual. The purpose of breaking-in is to transform a stiff, creaky hunk of store-bought leather into a hand-fitted, malleable, living extension of the hand. The kids in my neighborhood had all kinds of tricks for breaking in their gloves. They would put a softball in the pocket of a new glove, rub some oil on it, tie it up and leave it that way for a few days—a kind of Hoodoo trick to show ol'-man-glove what his business was. Later on, they'd unwrap it, whack it, spit on it, fold it, and trample it to shake the kinks out. They'd nurture it through its first games, getting familiar and finally intimate with it, pounding the pocket with a fist until it got used to the slam of the kid's knuckles and the sweat of his palm. You didn't borrow another kid's glove. You didn't even ask. That glove was his arsenal. He didn't part with it. He didn't tell you how he broke it in. That would be like the CIA giving away a secret code.

I'm told that spitting and thomping are no longer *de rigueur,* and the pros use a more persuasive approach in coaxing a glove to life. Richard Flaste, a tough investigative

The average softball glove contains 5–7 square feet of cowhide and about 100 inches of rawhide.

reporter for the New York *Times,* discovered the secret from informed sources and revealed everything in an article published March 9, 1977. According to Flaste, the pros put a handful of hot water in the glove's pocket, rub it in, and get their resident fast baller to throw some stingers until the pocket takes a set. They also use my old sand-lot method: put a ball in the wet pocket, wrap up the glove, and let it dry slowly during the course of several days. (Don't, repeat, don't put it near a heater or in the sun, as the leather will crack if the glove dries quickly.)

After the glove has been molded, take a couple drops of castor oil and rub it all over the leather—but don't overdo it with the oil, or the glove will turn leaden and floppy. At Doc's County Sports shop, they recommend a brand-name item called Glovolium. Another compound called Lexel can be rubbed inside the palm to prevent cracking when the leather gets soaked with sweat.

Naturally the baseball world was surprised and shocked by Flaste's revelations, but by now the players have probably developed new methods to create the perfect glove—methods beyond anything we dreamed possible.

Uniforms and extras. If you're inclined to buy a T-shirt, it'll cost you a few dollars to get one with "Blizzard's Bar" written in indelible script across the back. For a team that's investing more heavily: a full uniform costs from $40, for a durable but unglamorous outfit, to $100 or more for the type of threads they sport in the major leagues. Baseball/softball shoes have rubber cleats or flat spikes, and they cost $15–$30. Shoes with rounded metal spikes aren't allowed. Spikes are hardly appropriate if you're a good-timer, but they're absolutely required if you're a hotshot.

A cap costs $2.00 or $3.00. Bubble gum is $.20. And you're ready to go.

Umpire. Well, you're *almost* ready. Not quite. Because you need an umpire. He (or she) may seem like an unnecessary impediment to anyone brought up on sand-lot softball, but this authority figure is absolutely necessary if you have anything at all riding on the game—a bat, a beer, a reputation, a friendship, or your overblown ego. An umpire comes at a small price considering the phenomenal amount of ill-will he has to shrug off during a season. In exchange for your measly two bits, this umpire will hover behind the catcher in a hands-on-knees position, wearing a dark blue uniform and a mysterious belt-pouch containing scorer, measuring tape, pad, pencil stub, and aspirin, with a whisk broom protruding from his back pocket. He will call balls and strikes, tell the pitcher (in slow pitch) whether he or she is delivering the ball slowly enough; will serve judgment on a number of close plays, call foul balls, fair balls, and infield flies; will decide whether or not the runner touched the base, deviated from the base line, or interfered with a thrown ball; and will dust off home plate. If you abuse or threaten him after a warning, or punch him in the nose, he will throw you out of the game, which will be precisely what you deserve for behaving in such a manner.

An umpire can also teach you a thing or two. For example, Nancy was a very contented pitcher for the Knopf publishing company team in the publishers' league until she played against *Ms.* magazine. The ms.'s of *Ms.* wanted an official umpire, so Nancy found herself pitching for the first time under the scrutiny of a critical expert. After the first inning, the umpire (female) approached Nancy and said, "Listen, dearie, you're pitching way too fast for these babes." It was the first time in her modest pitching career that Nancy had been confronted with the slow-pitch rule. She was aghast and offended, but she learned something.

There's an old saying in the softball world which, like most old sayings, is pretty useless, but here goes: "The umpire is always right."

That's an exaggeration, of course, since no one is always right, but you have to pretend he is; otherwise, you could spend the rest of your softball life tied up in disputes. If you really don't feel like hiring an umpire, it's a good idea to appoint someone—player, bystander, or even your friend's father—to serve as an authority. Just make sure it's someone who can take abuse. Seeing an umpire cry is an awful thing.

Rules. Before you start to play, it's absolutely essential to know at least 50 per cent of them. If you have any doubts, just make up a rule—but get the other team to agree to it beforehand.

Of course, you can't anticipate everything. I saw a game in Central Park between the WCBS All-Stars and the Seven Lively Arts teams in the Show Business League, where a totally unexpected situation arose, and even the presence of a well-intentioned umpire wasn't much help. You see, there's a big tree in right field in diamond four at the Heckscher playground. Now, the umpire made it clear that any ball hit into the tree was an automatic double. But in the fourth inning, a hefty WCBS player came up to bat and, sure enough, hit it into the leafy arbor. He went two bases, then glanced over his shoulder and took a third. The right fielder for Seven Lively Arts made a lively delivery to the second baseman, who screamed, "HE'S AAOOOWT!"

Wuzzee? Did the rule mean he got two bases automatically, no matter what? Or did it mean he got two bases, with jeopardy? If the base was automatic, then he was safe even if he went farther. If it was a base with jeopardy, then he could be put out for going to third.

Obviously, there was only one solution. Squabble. So that's what they did.

PITCH AND HEAVE

The slow pitch. A slow pitch is an undistinguished sort of pigeon that leaves the pitcher's hand with a bit of flapping, takes a long low flight about 6 or 7 feet above the ground and lands gracefully in the catcher's mitt, having done its duty and no more. Here and there, you'll find a slow-pitch hurler who can make things a bit tricky for the batters. It's possible to change pace enough to worry the man at the plate: for instance, following a low, brisk pitch with a high-arching slow ball might induce him to swing too soon. If the arch is high enough and the ball falls late, it might be hard for the batter to tell whether it's going to be a ball or a strike before it crosses the plate. But do what you will, slow pitch remains a game for the hitters, and the pitcher must assume that his fielding job is just as important as the pitching.

At the start of the windup, you should stand on the plate with the ball held in front, and feet spread, ready for the forward step. Swing your arm back to a "nine o'clock" position, not above the level of the shoulder, with the elbow straight. Then, swing the arm down and forward, passing about 6 inches

Grip: Hold the ball loosely between thumb and four fingers. Release ball from fingertips, giving it forward spin.

from the hip. The ball is released below hip level and must travel at a moderate or slow speed, determined by the umpire. One foot must remain in contact with the pitching plate until the ball leaves the hand. The rules call for you to throw the ball in an arc at least 3 feet above the point of release, but not more than 12 feet above the ground. Again it is up to the umpire to judge what's acceptable. He may award the batter a ball or a base on a pitch that's too fast, and if the pitcher continues to throw deliberate fast balls, he can be taken out of the game.

As soon as the ball is released, the pitcher must throw his gears into reverse and back up right away, keeping his eyes on the ball. There's a good chance the batter will smash a fierce one down the middle, and the pitcher will have a much better chance of snagging the ball and/or protecting himself from sure death if he has backed up a few yards toward the outfield. Most slow pitchers do this automatically on practically every pitch.

It's not on the up and up to hesitate during the pitch, but sometimes a pitcher will precede a dull lob with an excess of energetic motion, to throw the batter off. It's also useful to put backspin on the ball, as a spinning ball will have a tendency to roll off the bat toward the ground.

To give the ball backspin, turn the back of the hand toward the batter. With some wrist action, you can get it spinning on the release, and it will keep whirling as it moves

toward that 200-pound mountain of muscle. Maybe, just maybe, he'll smash it into your glove instead of out to the back fence. If you're real lucky.

Fast pitch. In fast pitch the motivation for and execution of the pitch are infinitely more complicated. All the pitches used by expert baseball players, and then some, are possible in the fast-pitch softball game—including rise, drop, curve (inshoot and outshoot), the knuckle or slow ball, and the change-up. In addition, the heroic pitcher must worry about the strengths and weaknesses of each batter, pay attention to the catcher's stealthy signals, and notice the bad-mannered runner on first who is trying to steal second.

In fast pitch, according to the Official Rules, there are only a few restrictions governing the windup and delivery. Before pitching, the pitcher must "present the ball"—come to a complete stop facing the batter, with the ball held in both hands in front of the body. He can hold this position up to twenty seconds, with both feet in contact with the pitching plate, before beginning the windup. Then the ball must be delivered underhand, at any speed, with a single step forward toward home plate. Once the pitching motion has started, the pitcher is not allowed to stop, hesitate, or reverse the windup. In delivering the ball, he is allowed one long step toward the batter, and the back foot (pivot foot) can leave the pitching plate as soon as the forward foot touches the ground.

The best way to learn the fast pitch is to find some hotshot pitcher to teach you. Most instructors have techniques that are peculiarly their own, so it's best to find one and stick with him awhile, till you've figured out whether his style suits you. But fast-pitch twirlers aren't so easy to find these days, and maybe they'd just get impatient with you anyway. So, in the absence of a hotshot instructor, you can go out to your back yard and practice by yourself. Here's where you start:

The windup. There are four basic windups—windmill, figure eight, slingshot, and a hybrid called the "modified pitch." The windmill, as we all know, is a Dutch energy-saving device that utilizes wind to pump water out of the canals and into the fields. Applying this apt analogy to softball: your arm is the sail, and your poor ball-and-socket joint is at the hub of the wheel.

Suppose, for the sake of illustration, you're a right-hander. While standing on the plate, raise both arms in front, with the ball in the pocket of the glove. Bring your right hand, carrying the ball, over your head and around in a complete circle, while you lunge forward toward home plate. You whirl the ball around

Pitcher must "present the ball" before the windup; face the batter with both feet in contact with the pitching plate and the ball held in both hands.

once and release it near the thigh.

The power of the pitch comes from the whirligig routine, and if you've got a shoulder like the famous Shifty Gears (cf.) or Eddie Feigner (cf.), this is the windup for you. However, it may be difficult to control, and if you hear a snap, crackle, and pop coming from the neighborhood of your shoulder, give

Windmill 1. At the start of the windmill, weight shifts to rear foot.
2. Step forward as arm comes around the windmill turn.
3. Release ball just at the thigh or slightly in front. Many pitchers actually hit the thigh with forearm as they come through.

Figure eight 1. To begin the figure eight, swing the ball away from the side of your body, turning toward third base.

2. Bending the wrist and elbow, sweep the ball around behind your back.

3. On the release, snap your wrist as you bring the ball forward. Whiplike motion gives the ball added spin.

it up—your humerus is turning into Rice Krispies.

Seen from the batter's point of view, the windmill is an intimidating sight. Don Quixote, you will recall, thought he was fighting a whole army when he tilted at windmills. Faced with a windmill pitcher, batters may have the same delusion.

The figure-eight windup consists of a forward-and-back swing with complications. From the starting position, bring the gloved ball forward and upward. Then, as you make the step, sweep the ball back, carrying it well away from your body. Bend the elbow and wrist, scoop the ball around behind you, then release it with a flip of the wrist near your thigh.

On the figure eight, it's important to bend the elbow sharply and twist the wrist, so the ball is released with a kind of snap as your arm falls into line again. If it doesn't fall into line, your arm may stay in a pretzel position forever, so you should know the name of a good osteopath. Even the devotees of the figure eight (there aren't many) admit that the out-and-in sweep of the hand is a bit unnatural, so don't be surprised if you have trouble. And before you get wrapped up in that, here's a third variety that some experts consider the best of all:

It's called the slingshot. The windup is a simple back-and-forth motion. As you step forward, the right hand swings way, way back, higher than the shoulder, then down, forward and through, releasing the ball just in front of the thigh.

Slingshot 1. Bring gloved ball back along side, twisting body toward third base.
2. As weight shifts to rear foot, right hand swings back high above shoulder.
3. Leap forward as you fire the slingshot, throwing weight to left foot.

The slingshot allows for control as well as brute speed, and it's probably the easiest to learn.

There's a fourth windup that's used in games of "modified fast pitch." No windmill, figure eight, or slingshot are allowed in this game, nor can the pitcher make a complete revolution in delivering the ball. All he can do is bring the arm straight back and straight forward, keeping the wrist locked and elbow straight while he faces the batter. It's close to the slingshot but without the whipping motion, so the pitcher can't throw as fast. Also, in modified pitch, since the pitcher can't snap his wrist, it's difficult for him to put any stuff on the ball.

In a normal fast-pitch game, any kind of windup—windmill, figure eight, or slingshot —may be used effectively. There are certain advantages to each one, but the windmill is probably the most popular. The main thing is

to use the pitch that seems most natural and allows you to deliver the goods. Here are the goods:

Fast ball: A vicious straight-on pitch that's known for its velocity. Every hotshot seems to prefer a different grip on the ball— and a lot depends on the size of your hand— but the idea is to catch the ball in a kind of tripod, gripping it tightly between the thumb and middle fingers. Move your pinkie around so it will either help your control or else stay out of the way.

Slingshot pitchers release the fast ball with a forward-rolling motion of the hand and wrist—so the ball is snapped out between the spread thumb and forefinger. This gives the ball spin, which adds to the speed and, like a gyroscope, makes your satellite fly on course. The ball moves faster than you drive on the turnpike, so it's a good idea to practice awhile before endangering the bean of a living batter.

Fast ball 1. As arm swings down, turn the wrist in the direction of the pitch.
2. This gives the ball spin, so it flies straight with speed. Depending on the direction of spin, ball may curve right or left.

It's also important to release the ball low, as you'll lose control if you release it on the upswing. A few pitchers have been able to throw almost unlimited fast balls for many games, but they were mostly gods, and mere mortals like you and me will have to vary the routine with other pitches just so the golden arm doesn't tire.

Slow ball or *knuckle ball:* A pitch that floats through the air without spin and wobbles unpredictably as it comes over the plate. Because of this wobble, the batter will have a hard time finding it, and the catcher may too. It's a hard pitch to control. Furthermore, if the batter does connect, you're in trouble, since the spinless ball is easy to clobber.

To throw the knuckler, grip the ball between thumb and pinkie, with the left-over fingers knuckled under or (if your hand is small) pressing lightly against the hide of the ball. In effect, your hand is behind rather than under the ball, pushing it forward. It helps if you can hold the ball fairly loosely and release it from all the fingers at the same moment, so it travels without spin. It also helps to wear an innocent expression on your face, so the batter doesn't know what you're up to.

Rise ball: With this pitch the ball has a

Knuckle ball 1. Hold the ball loosely, well up in the palm with knuckles pressed against lacing.
2. On release, knuckles and palm push the ball forward without spin.

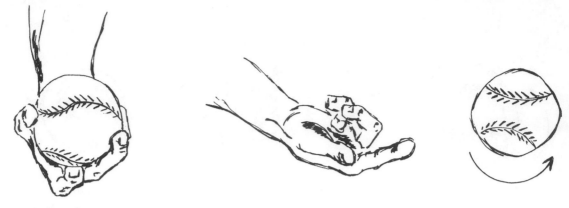

Rise ball 1. Forefinger is pressed against seam of the ball, with hand cupped underneath.

2. On release, push forefinger against lacing to make the ball spin backward.

backspin, so it takes a nasty cut upward as it crosses the plate.

Hold the ball with palm facing forward, thumb and pinkie pointed upward, and the forefinger tucked under or pressed against the lacing. The back of the knuckles are directed toward the batter on release. As you deliver the ball, push sharply with the forefinger so the ball develops a backspin. Served with moderate speed, the backspin on the ball causes it to break upward.

Now consider, from the batter's point of view, just how obnoxious this is. He sees the ball coming in at hip level, at reasonable speed. In other words, an easy home run. At the last second, the ball starts to shoot up-

ward, and by the time the chump has his bat around, the ball is breezing past him at shoulder level. He feels like a fool and looks like one too.

Drop ball or *sinker:* An opposite and equally evil effect is gained by getting the ball to drop from shoulder height to waist height in a flash.

The idea is to give the ball some forward roll as it leaves the hand. With the underhand motion, that kind of spin comes naturally. Grip the ball with the palm up, thumb on the outside, and a couple of fingers cradling it underneath. The ball is released on the upswing (but while the hand is still low), so it rolls off the middle fingers.

Drop ball 1. Hold the ball very tightly, with fingers across the seams.

2. When ball is released, "pinch" the seam with the bottom two fingers, so the ball starts to spin.

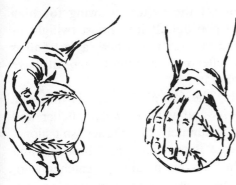

Change-up 1. Ball is gripped in the palm of the hand, with the fingers wrapped loosely around it.
    2. As the arm swings forward, turn hand over with palm downward.
    3. Release ball from the palm of the hand, using wrist action to give it the desired spin.

The real key to this pitch is in the follow-through. The hand comes up in a direct line as the ball is sent on its way with forward rotation. Where the ball drops will depend on the length of the pitcher's stride and where he releases it.

Change-up: This pitch is used like the knuckle ball for a change of pace, but while the ball travels at a slow speed, it has enough spin on it to move up or down. Combination of leisurely pace and some rise or drop make this a difficult pitch for the batter to meet—especially if he's expecting to shake hands with a fast ball.

The pitcher should conceal the ball in his glove while changing his grip, since the way he holds the ball is a giveaway to the batter. Hold the ball well up in the palm of the hand rather than in the fingers. The ball is released with the hand turned downward.

Curve ball: Some softball pitchers avoid this completely, since it can play into the batter's strength if it goes wrong. Therefore, the curve is usually wedded with a rise or drop, a combination of spins that can be murder on your arm but will give the batter fits.

The grip is the same as for the fast ball. On releasing the ball, however, the pitcher gives the wrist a smart snap in a clockwise or counterclockwise direction, so the ball has rotation toward or away from the batter. And that's the way it curves. The batter sees it coming in like a normal fast pitch, but at the crossroads it takes the path less traveled by, and sneaks way out toward the edge of the strike zone.

If a right-handed pitcher throws an in-shoot, the ball is rolled out between the thumb and forefinger in a clockwise direction. If you put enough on it, the batter will find himself swinging at a ball that's actually way inside, and he'll hit it with the narrow part of the bat. Not much power there. You just pick up his pitiful grounder, and throw him out at first.

Combinations. The basic pitches are used in various combinations, and this is where skill at bamboozling the batter is important. Every pitcher and every batter have individual strengths and weaknesses, and part of the fast-pitch game is out-psyching the man at the plate. One method is the change of pace: following two fast pitches with a knuckle ball or a low curve with a rising curve. But the pitcher has to know he can hit the target if he's playing on the weaknesses of the hitter.

For instance, if the pitcher is "jamming" a hitter—pitching in close where the ball will meet the small part of the bat—he has to be careful not to pitch a few inches out, where the big part of the Bombat will send the ball bombing toward the fence. Leonard Koppett, author of *All About Baseball,* points out that most big league pitchers are taught to err in the right direction, in case they miss the target. A low, inside pitch that goofs and goes through the middle will give the batter the chance he wants. Make it a little too far inside, and he'll be sure to have trouble with it.

The fast-pitch demon also has to keep a cluster of factors in mind—the count, the runners on base, and even the weather. If the count is 3–1 (3 balls, 1 strike), the pitcher is "behind" and needs to pitch a no-nonsense strike to put the batter in jeopardy. If the count is 0–2 (no balls, 2 strikes), the pitcher can tempt the batter to swing like crazy for a screwball that's way outside. Many pitchers use an in-and-out pattern as well as change of speeds, hoping a batter will swing wide for an inside pitch, or vice versa. And it's a rare circumstance when a pitcher throws three in a row of the same kind.

Since stealing is part of the fast-pitch game, the man on the mound must be ready for a quick throw to first, and he has to work with the catcher so that he doesn't serve an unexpected pitch that will get away. He should also be aware of the wind and lighting. With a strong wind coming in from the outfield, or in a field with a long fence, the pitcher can get the batter to swing for high pitches and pop out. If it's almost twilight or overcast and the lighting is bad, a fast ball is likely to be effective since the batter will have trouble seeing it.

Signals. The fast-pitch scene is indeed a battle of wits and wills between pitcher and batter, but fortunately the pitcher isn't alone. Every Charlie Brown has his Schroeder, and every pitcher has his invaluable catcher who, squatting down, flashes signals by tapping one, two, or three fingers against his inside thigh. Signals can get so elaborate that they're worse than Greek, but here are four that even Charlie Brown would understand: one finger for a fast ball, two for a drop ball, three for a rise, and four for a change-up. Simple enough.

But we live in a world of spies, and once the other team catches on, the pitcher has to start thinking of a new code. Maybe the catcher will flash one finger, then two, then one. It could mean a fast ball or a drop, and if the team at bat has a wise guy spying from the stands, he'll have to figure that out.

The pitcher may also "shake off" a pitch if he disagrees with the catcher's signal. But sometimes the "shake off" is just another elaborate ploy to confuse the batter. If the pitcher and catcher are having a lot of disagreements, or if they just feel like chatting about the weather, the catcher will come out to the mound and kick the dust around while the two cohorts mumble reassuring things to each other. Occasionally, the manager joins in. Then they all go back to their positions, with communications restored, and wipe out the team at bat.

THE SWING, THE SWAT, AND THE SLAM

In fast pitch, there's no doubt about what the batter's trying to do. Move the ball. By some means—desperate, shrewd, or crooked—he's got to make contact with one of those exasperating pitches and move the ball from home plate out toward the field. And that's tough when it's a fast ball clocking 90 mph.

In slow pitch, on the other hand, he has to be more selective about the kind of hit he wants to launch. Some home-run hitters will go for the fence every time, no matter what the out or inning. A great idea, of course, but if the ball falls short, his hit will be an easy out.

A more judicious batter will look for holes in the infield. Is the shortfielder playing to right or left of second? Is the third baseman missing grounders today? Then the batter will try to drive it through the infield with a line drive or a grounder. The goal of the medium hitter is to get a solid hit that will give him one or two bases. Let a powerhouse drive him home.

In both slow pitch and fast pitch, the advice from the experts boils down to a simple formula: Do what comes naturally, and then improve on it.

Hitting that ball is a natural reflex action. It's natural to watch the ball, and to try to hit it with the thickest part of the bat. The swing, shift of weight, and twist of the body on follow-through are all natural movements —and if all goes well, you'll hit the ball as deftly as William Tell pierced the apple.

But of course, you don't always hit well, and there may be things you can improve. Perhaps you're trying too hard for a home run. It's nice to have the kind of stroke that could kill a rhinoceros, but a softball has about 1/4000th the mass of a rhino, and if you don't develop accuracy, you won't be touching any bases all season long.

Maybe you aren't watching the ball carefully enough. This sounds elementary, but if your Uncle Duncan, who's just beginning on his second six-pack, is waving to you from right field, it can be damned distracting—so distracting that you miss the pitch. Forget him, the dope, forget the rude remarks of the first baseman, the noise of the crowd, the numbers on the scoreboard, and that awful breakfast you had. Just concentrate on the ball, the pitcher, and the instrument in your hands.

Other tips from the experts. Keep your chin tucked in near your shoulder, looking straight at the pitcher, so when you swing for the ball, your head doesn't move. (That's just another reminder: eyes on the ball, kid!) Keep the elbows away from the body so they don't go jamming you in the ribs when you try to swing. If your position at the plate seems to

Harold Kelley, slow-pitch slugger, demonstrates his home-run style. Toothpick is optional equipment.

cause trouble, try an "open stance"—standing almost erect rather than crouched, and turning so you half-face the pitcher.

Finally, don't swing up at the ball. It's a good way to slice air, but no way to get a 2-inch bat to confer with a 12-inch ball. In slow pitch, the batters used to perform a chop —coming down on the ball to make it bounce in front of the pitcher—but that's no longer allowed. However, there's nothing to stop you from swinging in a downward direction, and if you're doing everything else right, you just might come to terms with that hunk of leather.

Hitting a fast ball, or a fast pitcher's fancy stuff, naturally gives you headaches. Even if the pitcher isn't throwing a beanball (which is the quickest way to get a headache), you've got the problem of hitting a ball that

gets to you about half a second after it leaves the pitcher's hand. If the ball is a curve, rise, or drop, it probably won't be your favorite birthday gift, but you still have to try to open it up into a single or double. Of course you hope he'll throw it low and outside to your favorite smasheroo spot, but three hopes is the same as three misses. You can't wait forever. Take what comes and make the best of it.

Many coaches will advise a batter to "go with the pitch." This means that if a ball is pitched down the middle, hit it right back up the middle and make that pitcher hop. If the pitch is outside and you're a right-hander, just grab it and send a message over to right field, where it really wants to go anyway. An inside pitch is annoying, but if you can twist a bit as you bring the bat around, you might convince the ball to do some hard traveling down the third-base line. Then drop your bat and make like a locomotive.

In fast pitch, you're allowed to bunt, and there are good reasons for doing it. A "sacrifice bunt" will give a runner a chance to move from first to second or second to third—putting him in a better position to score. A well-placed bunt can be as good as a hit, and a fast runner can often get to first before the ball. Against a powerful pitcher, it may be very difficult to get any kind of hit at all—and a bunt is certainly better than nothing.

To execute the bunt, turn to face the pitcher as soon as he releases the ball. Move the upper hand along the bat. Block the ball as it comes over the plate. It's not a punch or a swing—just a matter of putting that big stick in the way. When you get to be a bunt specialist, you should be able to place it right between the pitcher and third baseman, where they'll bump heads and stay dizzy for the next three innings.

A team manager will put his power hitters near the top of the batting order, where they'll fill the bases and—if all goes well—drive in runs in the early innings of the game. There's a phenomenon that occurs in slow pitch, especially, that might be called a "hitting streak." Maybe it's the law of averages at work, but more likely it's a team aggression breaking loose. Suddenly, batters start to smash home runs. Excitement mounts, the spectators go nuts, and the team turns into a power station generating energy. It's wonderful to see.

Yogi Berra once complained that it was impossible for him to hit and think at the same time, but it's important to have some ideas about hitting before you get to the plate. You have to consider whether it's best to aim a grounder for a certain part of the field, hit a sacrifice fly (you're out, but the runners advance a base), bunt, or go for the low grounder through the infield. That all depends on the number of outs, players on base, and what you can get off the pitcher.

Also, you've got to know the strike zone. It's a lesson learned through many games—and from many umpires' calls—but without that lesson, you're at the pitcher's mercy. You'll go off-balance reaching for balls that are way outside, or stand and stare as a fast one whistles through the strike zone. And with the umpire howling "striiiiike taaawwooooo," you'll get so addled, you might stop thinking altogether. Never mind what Yogi says; you gotta think.

Chapter 4

A FIELD DAY

SOME ADVICE

If you're going to play the field, get a glove. That 12-inch ball is just too hard to catch in your bare hands, and often it's coming at you too fast. Besides, everyone else is going to have a glove, so why shouldn't you? The only exception is in 16-inch slow pitch, where the ball—16 inches in circumference—is sluggish enough and big enough that you can usually catch it with bare hands.

In each position the fielder has a particular kind of job to do, but it all boils down to a catch and a throw. The throw is almost invariably overhand, unless it's a situation where the fielder is close to the baseman and can flip it to him underhand. A good infielder scoops up the ball, straightens, winds up, and throws all in one split-second motion.

In fielding, the player must watch the ball every second (that old bugbear) and get as much of his body in the way as possible. This means standing squarely in front of the ball, with glove ready, and if that doesn't take guts, I don't know what does. On a grounder the glove is pointing down between the legs, and

you're ready to move it up quickly if the ball should take a nasty bounce.

When you've trapped the ball, straighten up as you recover and throw to the baseman. If you try to throw from a crouched position, the motion is awkward, and you'll sacrifice speed. Throwing sidearm may cause the ball to drop or curve on its way to the base. Watch any hotshot game and you'll see how it's done —making the catch, the windup, and the throw all in one motion. You'll also see, eventually, one of those spectacular catches where the shortstop makes a flying leap, catches the ball on a somersault, hops to his feet spitting dust, and fires it to first for an out. Maybe you can do that too, but remember, in any play like that, there's an element of luck as well as a large dollop of skill. You're better off being in the right place at the right time, if you can manage it: then relax, let the ball come to you, and scoop it up. When you make the throw, don't pay any attention to the runner— just look at the target, take aim, and fire.

To catch a line drive, put your glove up

in front of your chest and prepare for death calmly. Have your other hand next to the glove, ready to trap the ball. Don't blink. Don't wince. Your only chance of survival is to keep your eye on the ball.

Same goes for catching flies, but in this case you want to get under the ball. It's not advisable to hold your glove out stiff-arm and hope the ball finds it. While it may be against your instincts, you have to catch the ball near your body. Hold your glove and hand in a cup-shape position, trap the ball, and bring it in. The ball has spin on it, and you have to stop the spin at the same time you're catching it. Then fetch it out and send it to the infield.

Often the catch, recovery, and throw occur faster than the time it takes for a spectator to swallow his gum. So you hardly have time to think about where the runners are or where you should throw the ball. Think about that in advance. If you're playing shortstop and there's a man on first, you'll have two choices if the ball comes your way—throw it to second or first. If it's a speedy grounder, you might be able to zip it to second base to pick off the lead runner and try for the double play. But if the ball takes a long hop, the man at second is probably already safe—you might as well hustle the ball over to first base for one out. By the time you catch the ball, you should already know where you're going to throw it. Otherwise you'll waste precious seconds dithering around.

If you goof it up, just keep going. Everyone makes mistakes, you klutz, so just find the ball, pick it up, and throw. Don't panic. Don't get wild. If it's too late, well, that's a shame. Just hold on to the ball and accept the razzing. Whatever you do, don't throw it away.

Each position has its particular pleasures, duties, and requirements. You may have to shop around awhile before you find your *metier,* but here's a brief guide to ball-field employment.

Pitcher. In addition to the underhand duties already discussed, he has to get in the way of line drives, stop hitting streaks, and argue with the umpire. He'll cover first base if the first baseman takes an excursion to snag a right-field fly or grounder, and in fast pitch, the pitcher has to work with the first and third basemen to pick up the bunted ball. In watching for the steal (fast pitch only), he must keep one eye on the catcher, an eye on the baseman, and an eye on the thief. That makes three eyes. He's not allowed to "balk"—that is, pretend to throw to the base—but he can look in that direction as often as he likes, and throw a couple just to keep the runner pinned to the base. In slow pitch, of course, he's among honest peasants and needn't worry about stealing.

Catcher. The guy behind the plate doesn't have to run very far, but he must do practically everything else, from calling pitches to grabbing pop-ups and making that all-important tag-out at home plate. In fast pitch he has the added responsibility of hurling to first, second, or third to prevent a steal. Catchers are most frequently portrayed as being in the center of a cloud of dust, and that image is pretty accurate.

The catcher also has two important psychological jobs, for which no Ph.D. but good horse sense is required. He has to work well with the pitcher, particularly in fast pitch which is so much a pitcher-catcher's game. He's also the "holler man," the *basso profundo* of the team. Since he's the only one who can see the whole field, it's up to him to tell everyone else what to do. In a voice like God's. If he throws in a holler of encouragement along with his heap of advice, that's even better.

First baseman. In slow pitch the first baseman plays near the bag, but in fast pitch he moves in to be ready for the bunt. The first baseman doesn't need a great arm, but he should be able to stretch like an India rubber

One of the top fast pitchers in the country, Al Lewis plays for the Raybestos Cardinals, national champions in 1976. He was on the All-American team that year.

man to grab the throw. On a wild throw, the first baseman should stop the ball even if that means leaving the base. Otherwise, the ball will be lost in the bullpen, and the runner will sprint for second.

If it's a good throw, just keep your foot on the bag, glove up, eyes open, and catch it. (If you miss the ball, everyone will jeer at you behind your back. And you don't want that, do you?)

Second baseman. He plays to the right of second along the base line, and he's called the pivot man because everyone depends on him to make the double play. He has to get to the bag, catch a throw, tag the base, turn, avoid the runner, and make a speedy throw to first. The worst danger is the malevolent runner, who may be barreling into the baseman's blind side while he's looking toward third base or left field. (That runner is often a wretch with the worst intentions who doesn't mind sending a mild-mannered pivot man flying into the dust.) A strong arm isn't absolutely necessary, since most of his throws are to first. But sometimes the second baseman has to pick up the relay from the outfield and shoot it home. That takes some oomph.

Shortfielder. In slow pitch this "tenth man" usually plays to the left of second if the batter is right-handed and to the right if the player is a lefty. He plays shallow outfield— deeper, if there are long hitters—and often he's as busy as the shortstop. He's an essential relay man on the throw from the outfield.

Shortstop. "The ideal shortstop leads a quiet life like the serpent—but when he strikes, he strikes." So said sportswriter Ted Shane. Furthermore, the shortstop is often a busy serpent. Since most batters are right-handed, they'll pull the ball toward left field, and it will travel somewhere between second and third base. By observing a hitter's previous performance, a shortstop may be able to position himself for the hit—but no matter

Tom Kramer, second baseman for Katomah's Deer Park Inn, scoops up a hard-hit line drive and wings the ball to first for the out—effectively coordinating a fearsome expression with a perfect toss.

what he does, he'll have to move fast to pick up a hard-hit grounder. He needs a good arm, too, if he's going to get the ball to first on time. He's regarded as the "tenor holler man," as he communicates with the outfielders, reminding them where to throw.

Third base. What's needed here is courage and a strong arm. In fast pitch the third baseman has to move in for the bunt, and if it turns out to be a line drive toward his teeth, he'll need a very quick glove or a superlative dentist. Often he has to make a long, accurate throw from the third-base neighborhood to first. There's a joke about the third-base position which isn't very funny: "If his chest holds out, he'll have a good season." You know what that means? It means he stops the ball with his chest, if he has to. Anything, just so it doesn't get by him.

Outfield. It's been said that most outfielders make the play in the first step, not the last. What that means is that you have to judge the hit and get moving if you want to get under the ball (or in front of it) in time. Some outfielders are so good they take one glance, start running like hell, and don't look again until they're ready to catch the ball. That's impressive. A guy like me, on the other hand, has to keep looking over his shoulder.

"The sun got in my eyes," is not an acceptable excuse. (I should know. I tried it once, and the first baseman on my team said, "So what?") "I tripped" is also no excuse. Somehow, you're supposed to look up and down at the same time. "I thought you had it" is less than no excuse. You're supposed to call for these things and then get to them. "I thought it was going over the fence" is the dumbest excuse of all. Even if it looks like a home run, you've got to get back there by the fence and wait for it, just in case it drops in. With any spunk at all, you'll climb the chain-link and reach like King Kong for the top of the World Trade Center. It's a lot of work, but if you make that miraculous catch, someone's going to buy you a whole keg of beer after the game.

Deprived of any decent excuses, the only alternative left to the outfielder is to make the catch. You'll get the hang of catching flies, and a grounder has usually mellowed out by the time it reaches the outfield, but a line drive can be a real stinker. Trouble is, most liners have some sort of curve to right or left, but you don't notice until the ball comes within range. By then it may have curved beyond hope. Nevertheless, you're expected to do the impossible. And then make an equally impossible throw—either to a relay man or right to the base.

Playing the outfield can be a lonely business—out there with no friends in sight and a bunch of hostile fans telling you your pants are falling down. In the dreary outfield of fast pitch, where there may be only one or two flies a game, the outfielder may fall victim to a dangerous syndrome known as "outfield blahs." His attention wanders. His eyes glaze. He's not sure which inning it is, which out, which day, which ball field. The sun is blazing hot. He feels slightly dizzy.

This is a serious disease. Some players pinch themselves. Others recite poetry. A few blow bubble gum. But these are merely stop-gap measures. The only real way to cure the outfield blahs is to get into the game again. Ask yourself: What is the pitcher doing? Where is the batter going to hit it? Where did he hit it last time? Where do I throw the ball?

Then, when it comes, you'll be ready for it. Or at least not completely asleep.

Some outfielders just can't resist the temptation to whistle, wriggle, and shuffle their feet. Witness Rita Moreno, actress, with a bad case of the outfield fidgets.

GOOD YELLING AND BAD YELLING

Suppose you're playing right field, with Andy in center, and this high fly ball looks like it's coming down right between you. Off the field, you and Andy may be very considerate, mild-mannered people with soft voices, but suddenly you find yourself doing something totally unexpected. You're yelling at Andy. Loudly. Authoritatively.

"IT'S MINE! I'VE GOT IT!"

Now, what you actually mean to say is: "Considering the trajectory of the ball and the wind velocity and my relative distance from the ball's probable landing site, the chances are nine in ten that I'll get to it before you get to it, so please stay out of my way, Andy."

But you don't have time to say all that, do you? You'd just about get to the word "trajectory" before you'd collide with Andy. You might both get concussions. You don't want that to happen. So you yell. Yelling is, without question, one of the most important factors in winning a softball game.

What you shouted at Andy is an example of an utilitarian yell. It was a warning and a commitment. It puts the burden of responsibility on your shoulders. If you don't get to the ball in time, you'll be in hot water with the whole team. But if you make the catch and avoid colliding with Andy, you'll be considered a pretty remarkable person.

There's also the spirited yell that doesn't do anything, exactly, but just kind of gets the team moving.

"Come on, Meatloaf, get a hit!" is an example of spirited yelling. It's what you yell when Meatloaf goes up to bat. When he lets a ball go by, yell, "That's it, wait 'em out. Pitcher's got nothin'!" If he swings and misses, you may have to resort to "Good cut!" which is pretty noncommittal, but at least shows you're still behind him all the way.

If Meatloaf gets a hit, you can change over to hoarse-voiced yelling. This doesn't have to be articulate, but should be combined with some body language, like waving your fists, hammering the bench or (if you're a manager), pacing nervously up and down in the front of the stands.

Besides utilitarian and spirited yelling, there's also advisory yelling. The catcher does a lot of this, coming out of the cage and bellowing, "Two out! Two out!" Or the third-base coach, as the runner comes around: "Keep going!" (Accompanied by a lot of arm motion.) Or the shortstop to an addled outfielder: "Throw to third!"

Yelling begins at an early age, but there are varying degrees of sophistication. Many kids still use the old stand-by: "Two-four-six-eight, pitcher's got a bellyache." But they can also be devastatingly blunt at times: "Ah, Stevie, you're a creep!" And a lot of kids still swear by the favorite, "I see England, I see France . . ." routine, but it doesn't do much damage any more. There is, however, the perspicacious observation, "You run like a duck."

If you've ever seen a duck run, you will realize just how awful this insult is.

Among adults, there are regional insults that can be curiously piquant, especially in national tournaments. Northerners get called "Damn Yankees" in the South, and Southerners earn the epithet "Cotton Pickers" up North. A team from Washington might be accused of being "a bunch of politicians" and a team from Cleveland will know what you mean when you say, "the mistake on the Lake." They won't like your remarks, either.

Occasionally, players become famous for their yelling. The Pittsburgh pitcher, Louis Delmastro, was renowned for following a player around the bases when he'd hit a home run. As the player loped around, Louis screamed insults about the team, the player, the manager, and the manner in which they were born. (This was the same Delmastro who once pitched his glove over the plate when he became irritated with an umpire. He was, of course, thrown out of the game.)

There is also the kind of yelling that kids and adults do to each other. A lot of this goes on around the stands. For instance:

"Hey, Dad, can I get a soda?"

"You don't need it. You just had one."

"My mouth's dry."

"Never mind. You don't need it."

Conversation continues until kid, inevitably, gets his soda.

In the field, the defensive team ("Big D, Big D, Big D!") has its own set of yells. The third baseman may shout "No batter! No batter!" just before the pitch, and the first baseman will add, "No stick at all! Lights out! Nothin' there at all!" These remarks are designed to make the batter feel about two inches tall. You might also hear the intimidating comment, "He's a looker!" It doesn't mean the batter is all that attractive—just that he "looks over" most of the pitches and hesitates on the swing.

On the offensive team, the idea is to support the batter and give him encouragement. Any student of ball-park shouting will notice immediately how many "Babes" step into the batter's box.

"Let's go, Babe, start it off!"

"This is the inning, Bernie Babe!"

"Way to look, Babe, way to look."

Once they return to the bench, of course, players resume their given names, and the colloquial "Babe" is dropped.

As the game progresses, yelling will inevitably become more intense. Sometimes it's not even clear what all the excitement is about, but as long as the noise continues, you can be sure the game is progressing satisfactorily.

"Come on, guys, let's go—let's rattle this man's cage!"

"Keep a look! Right on top! Let's go now!"

"Jump on these guys! Paddle this man!"

"You're so far out the mailman can't find you!"

"Here ya go, Sammy. A little bingo. Little bingo!"

"Look at 'em! They're a bunch of criers!"

"Not a chance! They're down! They're down now!"

"Full count! Let's go, full count!"

And then comes the best yell of all:

"WEEEEE WOOOOOOOON!"

THE ART AND ANARCHY OF ARGUMENT

As will be apparent to anyone who has ever watched or taken part in softball, The Argument is an essential element in the game. Consider, for instance, the unique pleasures of the Argued Play. You can go along quite reasonably for five innings or so, cheering the good hits, yelling out your team support, grumbling about the umpire—the usual sort of thing—but somehow you feel like the game isn't quite lively enough. Something's lacking. Something intangible—but so essential to the game, you don't feel complete without it. And then it happens. In the bottom of the third, the top of the fifth, or on the dangerous precipice of the seventh, it strikes without warning: The Big Argument.

The disputed play is sometimes very complicated. Did the second baseman have his foot on second when he made the pivot for the double play? Was it an infield fly, with less than two outs, and two men on base? (This is a toughy, by any measure.) Did the runner interfere with play by jabbing the shortstop in the ribs? I mean he whammed the guy right in the chest. Jees, he could have killed him! This is how it gets started. Sure, the umpire has already made his decision (if there is an ump), but everyone else on the field knows at once that this is a disputed play, and they throw themselves into the controversy with zest and venom. Everyone on the Toodlebogs team says, "By God, he was safe," and everyone on the side of Bill Bixby's Bar says, "Yer crazy. He was out." Now it's more than just coincidence that everyone on the offensive side, that is, the Toodlebogs, saw and will defend to the death the fact that their runner was safe. Also more than coincidence that every one of the BBB gang swears the runner was out. I mean, you don't find any crossovers, any of the Toodlebogs agreeing with the Triple-B's, or vice versa. That's funny—I mean odd. No it's not. It's teamwork. It's natural. You don't argue against your own team no matter what. Never mind what you actually saw, when the Disputed Play comes up, you go the way the team goes, and that's it. Lie if you have to, but don't be silent. Stand up and be counted.

No matter what play is disputed, you have to think of it as the deciding play of the game. If you win this argument, you're winning the whole game. Theoretically, of course. In point of fact, the damn out may be unim-

Arguing with the ump is traditional, but everyone looks a little bit tougher with hands on hips. Engaged in controversy are Gary Carroll of Howard & Carroll (Sherrill's Ford, N.C.) and umpire Robert Holder. Ron Patterson of Burnette & Associates (Chattanooga, Tenn.) looks on.

portant when measured against the twenty other outs that have to be made this game. But on the other hand, it could be the play that makes you or breaks you. You have to think that way if you're going to argue hard.

Of course, it's essential to argue hard. You start off by picking on the umpire. Suppose you're with the Toodlebogs, and the ump calls your player "Out!" You've got to jump on him right away. Open your mouth, take some air in your lungs, and bellow good and loud, "AAAHHH, UMP, YERRR CRAZY." After that opener, you won't have to worry much about volume, because the guys from Bill Bixby's Bar will drown you out anyway. Their first baseman is gonna snap it up, turn to you with a superior grin, and say, "ARE YOU NUTS? THAT GUY WAS OUT BY A MILE."

Now you know and I know the guy wasn't out by a mile, he was out by inches if at all, but that's semantics, and you're arguing about a principle, so jump in there again.

"Ump, you couldn't even see that play!"

This is a good line in almost any situation. It puts the ump on the defensive because it means the play might really be in contention. And it gives you ample opportunity to point your finger and wave your arms. These are forceful, hostile gestures that let the opposition know just how emphatic you feel about this play.

The next move is up to the player in the field, and it can be extremely dramatic. The second baseman, seeing that there's about to be a conference called with the umpire, where *his* out might be disputed and taken away from him, suddenly invests every ounce of his ego in a ferocious shout and furious gesture.

"MY FOOT . . ." he yells, pointing to his foot, ". . . WAS ON THE BASE . . ." he continues, pointing to the dusty bag, ". . . AND HE NEVER CAME CLOSE!" He flings down his glove and stalks across the field, gulp, in your direction. It looks like trouble all the way.

Now, as anyone can see, the discussion is fraught with emotion, and the whole situation shows complete disregard for the niceties of a parliamentary system. But it's the softball way of settling things.

Every person has preferences, and different teams argue in different ways. I have seen, for example, a twelve-year-old first baseman pick up a nine-year-old runner and forcefully replant him several yards from the base itself. Kids of this age may also be prone to dispute with their own players. One occasionally sees a young pitcher throw his glove at a second baseman, calling him a "stupid toad" for committing some totally innocent error. At a later age, the disputes are largely verbal rather than physical, but you must admit, any runner who intentionally spikes a third baseman must have a foul, surly streak in his nature.

Women rarely engage in hair pulling, scratching, or biting—no, in softball, women throw punches. If it comes to that.

It rarely comes to that, either among men or women, because the umpire usually manages to rule the field as he (or she) should. But it should be emphasized that a real combatant can argue about anything. You can argue about what position you have to play. You can argue about who buys the beer. You can argue about who made the error when the shortstop threw to first. You can argue about who should have caught the fly in the outfield. You can argue about arguing.

It's one reason softball is so popular.

BEER

Beer, as we all know, has traditionally been associated with softball, and along with arguing and yelling, may have something to do with its extraordinary popularity across the land. It's true that you don't *have* to drink beer to be a successful and amiable ballplayer (unless your sponsor happens to be a bartender who will be very insulted if you don't try whatever he has on tap). There are lots of softball players who don't drink beer. I know a kid in Baltimore, Sammy Evans, who's a pitcher for the Cobblestone School team. He's eleven years old, and he doesn't drink beer. He pitches pretty well, too. So, you see, it's not required.

But it's certainly a part of softball life, and besides how else are you gonna develop a really attractive paunch that you can rest your hands on in your old age. A paunch that has rotundity, dignity, and bulk. A paunch that's a companion and a source of comfort. True, you can do it with potatoes. But the experts, I mean the big guys we're talking about, do it with beer.

There are three types of beer drinkers: before-the-game drinkers, during-the-game drinkers, and after-the-game drinkers. Those who indulge before the game have a couple of things in mind. They realize that it's almost 98 degrees Fahrenheit out there on that field, which means they're going to lose a lot of body fluids during the game. It would be unwise and dangerous for a trim young fellow of fifty-five, weighing a mere 231, to perspire freely in all that heat without having something in reserve. This fellow's attitude toward beer is like a camel's attitude toward water. He is merely showing prudence and wisdom in visiting the watering hole before the game.

Of course, if he overindulges, he can't really be considered prudent or wise. In fact, filling up with too much beer may cause the player to weave in the outfield and bat crosslegged. It's true that a relaxed stance is advisable, but certainly not with the knees on the ground. And a crosslegged batting position puts unconscionable strain on the tendons. The before-the-game drinker, therefore, had better limit himself to what makes him buzz, and stop short of what makes him sink.

During-the-game drinkers are one and all a tough breed, and the rookie would be well-advised to watch his step around them. Frequently, a during-the-game drinker has an inflated sense of worth that becomes more inflated as the game rolls on. The first time he steps up to the plate, he thinks he's Mickey Mantle. The second time up, he'd swear he was Ted Williams *and* Mickey Mantle. The third time up, he really believes he's some extraordinary combination of Babe Ruth, Ted Williams, and Mickey Mantle all rolled into one. This self-image is due to the cumulative effects of the beverage that he's keeping under the bench. Meanwhile, also due to the beverage, his reflexes are slowing down. That

by it, even if we occasionally give the third baseman from the other team a punch in the nose. (After all, he deserved a punch in the nose, first for insulting your girl friend, and secondly for stomping on your right toe with his spikes.) Most of the time, though, we just stand around with these mugs in our hands that keep getting filled up and emptied almost miraculously. After a while, we're able to recall softball stories that aren't even true, and furthermore aren't even funny, but they sure seem hilarious. We're also able to consume huge amounts of hamburgers and french fries along with our beer. What we aren't able to do is drive home.

If you're an after-the-game beer drinker, it's a real shock to walk out into the bright sunlight from a dim bar. That's why many softball games are played at night. I've heard that there are wives of some softball players who say an after-the-game drink isn't necessary. These wives have what is called a bad attitude. They should realize that a softball game is only what you make of it. And you can't make anything of it unless you talk about it, and the time to talk about it is immediately after the game. That's when everyone has to get together and decide what the history-making version of the story is going to be. Early in the evening, Artie might say: "Did you see that home run? Three hundred and fifty feet at least." Everyone nods and agrees it was a helluva hit. Then about a half hour (and three beers) later, Joey speaks up and says, "You know that home run was four hundred feet, I'll bet." There's some argument about this statement, but by the time another round has been ordered, everyone has come to realize that it *was*, in fact, a 400-foot slam. It's only a matter of time before Karl, who hit the home run, speaks up and announces that the ball went 432 feet. "How do you know that?" someone asks. "I measured," says Karl. Well, the news travels pretty fast around the bar,

means, by the third time up, he's probably whiffing lob balls that any klutz in the Triple-A League could hit. At this point, the umpire's opinion of him ("YER OUT") will differ sharply from the batter's image of himself. Upon being called out, the during-the-game drinker may throw a fit. He may have to be carried out of the game in a strait jacket. But this is unusual. More commonly, he will shrug his shoulders more despairingly than they have ever been shrugged before, and try to find his way back to the bench. The batter on deck can help by pointing the way.

After-the-game beer drinkers are guys like you and me, and we don't mean any harm

"Sell two, drink one" is the policy of a concessionaire at Cleveland's Brookside Park. Ohio is renowned for its annual Stroh's softball tournaments, where the sponsor provides free beer.

and by the time everyone's ready to leave, they realize it's a red-letter day. Karl Bernakovsky has just set a new record for a home-run hit in Perlham Field.

There are also husbands who have a bad attitude. They believe that if a man has a beer, he's just having a good time with the fellas. But if a woman has a beer after the game, she's shirking her responsibilities to her family. It just so happens that a woman's responsibility after the game is first to her team and secondly to her family. If the team makes history, then she must celebrate.

Many players don't drink any beer at all. The courage of these players must be admired, but just think of the dangers! In the first place, there is the risk of staying in top-notch physical condition, with all the disastrous things that implies—running hard, keeping thin and muscular, improving your game. Also, there's the danger of taking the game seriously. If your team starts winning games at the local, state, regional, and national levels, you may suddenly find yourself playing for keeps. You might find yourself, at the end of the season, with a trophy in your hand. Then what do you do? I mean, where are you going to *keep* the damn thing?

The other danger of not drinking beer is that you may hurt softball sponsorship. I mean, if people don't drink beer, then bars are going to stop sponsoring teams, and then we wouldn't have all these softball fanatics pouring into the city's recreation parks. Also, you won't have Stroh's sponsoring the annual tournament, because why should they if no one drinks Stroh's. (In this regard, it should be mentioned that Coca-Cola and other soda companies have made terrific inroads into the softball field in the past few decades—awarding trophies and so forth—but have not yet been able to dislodge the primal beverage, beer.)

Whether or not players keep up their gross consumption, however, there will always be the spectators. The amount of beer consumed at annual tournaments by spectators has been described as "rivers." Now, if you go to a little game between Baptists and Methodists in a southern town, this isn't the case. In fact, it's a pristine business—no beer anywhere. But up North, the spectators smuggle it on the field one way or another. It's concealed in articles of clothing, in coolers, in paper bags and—in some cases—carried around openly just as if it were lemonade or something like that. The people who have been drinking it for a long time are really big, and usually they're really noisy, so you can always identify them. The people who are just getting started have a tendency to burp loudly. So you can identify *them* too. But if you got an early start before the game, and brought a six-pack along with you, it's unlikely you'll be able to identify anything or anybody with particular accuracy. So just lean back and enjoy the game. You're among friends.

Chapter 5

WOMEN'S CLOUT

THE REIGN OF JOYCE

It's a bad idea to get Ted Williams mad. He's got a fiery temper, and he's been known to wave his fists in the direction of someone's jaw when he's really irritated. Considering the temperament of the man, it's remarkable how well he took it, that day he was struck out by a female softball pitcher. In fact, he was struck out about ten times.

It was a sunny day in 1962, and the Police Department in Waterbury, Connecticut, had scheduled a charity softball game. The women's team from Stratford, the Raybestos Brakettes, was playing against another fast-pitch team. Ted Williams was invited to hit a few off of the Brakettes' pitcher, Joan Joyce. Just as a stunt.

Now, Ted Williams (who played for the Boston Red Sox) won the American League batting championship six times, was the last man in the league to hit over .400, and is a member of baseball's Hall of Fame—but he didn't do so well against Joan Joyce.

Williams was at bat nearly ten minutes, in front of a crowd of 18,000. Joan Joyce threw 40 pitches. She threw knuckle balls, screw-balls, fast balls, in-shoots, out-shoots, rise curves, and drop balls. Ted Williams managed to get one hit. He succeeded in banging another one into foul territory. But he couldn't touch the rest of her pitches.

"He was very upset," Joyce recalls, "and finally he threw down the bat and walked away."

It was perhaps unfortunate for Ted Williams that he had to face one of the greatest women's softball pitchers of all time. Joan Joyce is one of those creations commonly referred to as a "natural athlete." She plays volleyball and basketball, she's a championship golfer and bowler, and she can pitch. Oh, sister, can she pitch.

Joan began playing in 1955, when she was thirteen. Her father was a factory foreman and her mother a worker in a plant in Waterbury, Connecticut, and Joan used to fill in the after-school hours by pitching a ball against the wall of her house. Then she devised a "strike zone" made out of chicken wire stretched between two trees. Her father was a softball addict, and every night during the

Joan Joyce and the wicked slingshot. Brace yourself for a knuckle ball (left) and a fast ball (right).

summer he'd take his three kids out to the park to watch the softball games. Joan and her older brother ended up loving the game.

As a young teen-ager Joan joined up with the Raybestos Brakettes, fortuitously located nearby in Stratford, Connecticut. For the first few years of her career, Joan was a strong pitcher but she lacked control. The problem was with her windmill style. It was the only windup she knew, but many of her pitches went wild.

The break-through, she recalls, came during a practice when she was about eighteen. One day she was warming up at Raybestos Memorial Field, where some workmen were

stringing opening day banners around the telephone poles. One of the workmen climbed down the ladder, took a long look at Joan's pitching style, then asked her why she was using the windmill. When she told him it was the only windup she knew, the workman promptly put down his hammer and demonstrated the slingshot pitch for her. She tried it out, and it felt natural, so she stuck with it.

And that made all the difference. When the manager of the Brakettes saw the change in her style, he got Johnny Spring to come out and coach her. Spring was the hero of the Raybestos Cardinals, with a phenomenal record of victories. In 1958 he'd pitched the Cardinals (the men's team) to a championship in the nationals with a perfect no-hit, no-run game in the finals. Johnny showed Joanie the rise ball, the drop ball, and the change of pace. With the slingshot delivery, these pitches started to work and Joan's confidence took a sharp rise curve.

The Brakettes already had one ringer on their team—a formidable pitcher called "Blazin' Bertha" Tickey—and Joyce teamed up with her to win the national championships in 1958, '59, and '60 for the Brakettes. Blazin' Bertha was the best women's pitcher in the league. She had played first with the Orange, California, team (the Lionettes) and captured four national championships before joining the Brakettes in 1958. By the time she retired, at the age of forty-two, she had won a total of eleven national championships, been named eighteen times to the National All-Star Team, and was MVP eight times at the tournaments. Her lifetime record in twenty-three years of pitching was 757 won, 88 lost, with 162 no-hit, no-run games. When Joan joined forces with this big woman with swirling blond hair, the Brakettes team became virtually indestructible. That was before the Big Switch.

The Big Switch came in 1963, when Joyce left Stratford to go to college in California—and to play softball there. Her college residence was within commuting distance of the practice field of the Orange Lionettes. Joyce began pitching for the Lionettes, and the people of Stratford gritted their teeth. A showdown was bound to come.

Come it did. In 1964, on the opening night of the world championship, Joan Joyce hurled a no-hit, no-run game against her former teammates, and the Brakettes went down to a 2–0 defeat at the paws of the Lionettes. Dumped in the losers' bracket, the Brakettes fought their way through fifty consecutive scoreless innings, with Blazin' Bertha doing all the pitching. By the time they got to the final

"if" game, the Lionettes had been knocked out, and Bertha had to face Erv Lind's Florists of Portland, Oregon. The Brakettes lost, 1–0.

In 1965, it was again the Orange Lionettes, led by Joan Joyce, against the Raybestos Brakettes, equipped with Blazin' Bertha and a brilliant new pitcher, Donna Lopiano, in the finals for the National Women's Fast-Pitch Championship. The match was held at Stratford, and the final game between the Brakettes and the Lionettes went 12 innings. When the dust cleared, Joanie and the Lionettes had won.

Donna Lopiano pitched the heartbreaker for Raybestos. She later recalled, "Half the crowd was for Stratford and half wanted Joanie to beat us. Most of the bad feelings had worn off by then, but it was still awfully tough to lose to Joan."

In 1966 someone checked up on Joan's fast ball. It crossed the plate at 118 mph.

By 1967 Joyce had finished college and returned to the Stratford fold, and Raybestos had the combined artillery of four great pitchers—Joyce, Blazin' Bertha, Donna Lopiano, and Donna Hebert. They combined to grab 67 wins with only 2 losses for the season, and the Brakettes did not give up a single run in the national tournaments.

As an amateur, Joan Joyce won more than 400 games for the Brakettes. In the first eighteen years of her career she pitched 110 no-hitters and 35 perfect games. And in 1974 she led the Brakettes to victory over the Japanese team in the World Championship. In fact, there's only one thing wrong with this athlete. As Joan says: "It's boring to watch me."

But boring or not, she's the Sandy Koufax of women's softball, admired and well-liked by just about every woman player who's ever met her. Still going strong at the age of thirty-six, she stands 5'9", weighs 160 pounds, and is known as a shy person with a tremendous

The Raybestos Brakettes celebrate yet another victory. From 1958 to 1976 the women's fast-pitch team won twelve national championships.

desire to win. In 1976 when Joyce helped found the International Women's Professional Softball Association, she also organized the Connecticut Falcons, a team based in Meriden. She recruited most of the team from her alma mater, the Raybestos Brakettes. To no one's surprise, the Falcons quickly took the lead in the Eastern Division and faced off with San Jose's Sunbirds, who drew most of their talent from another amateur team, the Santa Clara Laurels. WPS instituted a rule that a pitcher can't appear in consecutive games, so Joyce was giving up the mound every other game to southpaw Sandy Fischer.

By the end of the season, Falcons and Sunbirds had met eight times, each winning four games. But the World Series went to the Falcons—easily. Joyce allowed only a few hits in the first game, then knocked in the first two Connecticut runs to win, 3–0. Sandy Fischer won the second, 4–2, and Joyce was back for the third. In the next-to-last game of the season, she allowed Cyndi Lillock of the Sunbirds to hit a home run over the left-field fence. It was the first earned run Joyce had given up all season. She struck out 7 of the last 12 batters, for a total strike-out record of 36 batters in 18 innings. The Falcons took the fourth and final game, 3–0, to end their grueling 120-game schedule.

A rival pitcher for the San Jose Sunbirds, Charlotte Graham, has faced Joan Joyce in dozens of games as an amateur and professional.

"She's a fantastic lady," Graham told a reporter. "She's my idol. I've watched her closely for ten years. She's truly the best player women's softball has ever had."

Considering Joan Joyce's record, that may be an understatement.

GIRLS' GUMPTION

Women's softball has frequently been considered a novelty item, and so-called "girls' games" are often considered a pale pink imitation of masculine softball. Obviously, the Raybestos Brakettes, the Falcons, and the Sunbirds don't fit into the pale pink category insofar as these teams play very serious, sometimes terrifyingly serious softball. But even the lesser women's teams, the starters in the sport, show a good deal of spunk, stamina, and gumption. If you don't believe it, all you have to do is take a walk in Central Park on a Monday evening, and watch the "girls" playing there.

The Center Recreation League of Central Park consists of a dozen girls' teams recruited from various businesses around the city. The "girls" in this case are women in the age range of eighteen to thirty who work for the sponsoring companies as secretaries, merchandisers, buyers, computer programmers, or managers and play softball on Tuesday evenings in two shifts, from 5:30 to 7:00, or 7:00 until sunset.

Bob Vassil, coach, instructor, general manager, and pep talker *extraordinaire,* raises a point of order with the ump. J. C. Penney, on the bench, backs him up.

In 1977 one of the new, promising teams in the Center Recreation League was sponsored by J. C. Penney. Penney's had a championship men's softball team (slow pitch) for four years in a row, and when the personnel department asked for suggestions for expanding the company's recreation program, the female employees voted overwhelmingly to have their own softball team. Accordingly, tryouts were held. One hundred twenty-six women showed up.

Bob Vassil, a right fielder for the men's team, agreed to oversee the tryouts and to serve as manager and coach for the women's team during its first year. A former baseball player who once upon a time tried out for a number of pro teams (including the Mets), Vassil wanted a team that would be serious about winning the championship, and he selected a team of twenty dedicated softball players.

Many of the Penney players had not been on a softball field since high school, but they started their spring practice a full month before the season began—getting their fielding experience in the chilly, wet weather of April. After the start of the season, the women came to Central Park every Thursday evening to watch the men's games and take fielding and batting practice afterward. On Mondays they would arrive early in Central Park to warm up before their games—which were played on an out-of-the-way corner diamond thickly surrounded by shade trees, with an outfield overgrown with weeds. By midseason, the rookie Penney team was second in the league, led only by the formidable veterans of Bristol-Myers. (Other teams in the league included: Arista Records, Burlington Mills, Pfizer Drug Co., A. C. Nielsen, Western Electric, the Environmental Protection Agency, Loews Theatre, Lever Bros., Caltex Petroleum, and Oppenheimer Company.)

Before each game, Bob Vassil calls his team to a long park bench and exhorts them to do their best and, for God's sake, to listen to him.

"Go out there and do your bit, and you're gonna come out on top," he says. "You've gotta be good, look sharp if we're gonna beat a team like Bristol. Okay? Now, I want more from the bench. You've gotta shout it out: 'Come on, Lydia! Come on, Ronnie!' And pay attention. You can't be out in the field singin' a tune and lookin' at the hotdog wagon 'cause that might be just the time the ball comes your way. Don't listen to the people behind the backstop. Listen to me. Okay? Tune out everyone but me. If you got a question, you run to me. Say, 'What do I do?' and I'll tell you. Okay?"

Before announcing the day's line-up, he apologizes for not being able to use everyone. "But you're all gonna get a chance," he says. "If not this week, then next week, or the week after that."

Having been encouraged to go out on the field and give their all, the Penney girls run through a brief warm-up while Vassil reviews a few field rules with the female umpire. A hit into the trees is only good for a double. One base on an overthrow. Slow pitch only, of course, and an out will be called on anyone who throws the bat. Since there's another game on the diamond at seven o'clock, the last inning must begin by 6:50. Otherwise, the game will be called by the ump, and the team that's ahead is the winner.

In the early innings, as Vassil feared, the yelling from the bench is tentative and *sotto voce*.

"Come on, Allison, get a hit. You can do it," declaims one of the girls, in a voice so quavery it's lost in the trees.

"Let's *hear* it!" roars Vassil. "COME ON, ALLISON, GET A HOME RUN NOW! Come on, bench, let's *hear* it."

After a while the bench is in full voice, and by the time Allison has scored her third run, the women from Penney's are yelling like crazy.

"All *right,* Allison," bellows Vassil. "Your name's gonna be first on that bulletin board."

The bulletin board, as they all know, is the one back at the office. During the week, the names of the leading batters are displayed there along with their averages. Being on the bulletin board constitutes a signal honor. In early season, the leaders included Gaylen Savage (Slugger Savage) with a .900 average, Rose Iacovelli (.688), Doris Doran (.647), and Marianne Graham (.517). Soon, it appears, Allison Heinjmann will be listed among the elite.

The spectators behind the bench and the backstop include some of the boys from the office and also some gentlemen visitors of Central Park who have followed the ups and downs of the Center Recreation League for

Gaylen "Slugger" Savage, leading scorer for J. C. Penney, raps out a double in a game against Lever Brothers.

the past four or five years. The gentlemen watch the game with an air of indulgence mixed with amusement, but they also express real respect for the women's enthusiasm and for the well-executed plays that occur frequently. In the CRL there are few players who field the ball with authority, but the women are absolutely serious about their game. Sometimes a fly ball is caught just at the top-end of a wavering glove. Sometimes a throw from shortstop to first base seems to take forever to complete its high arc. Sometimes a grounder escapes the fielder's glove and disappears far, far into the weeds of the outfield. But there's more danger to a game like this—where the simplest play may explode into a major disaster—and even the most bemused gentleman spectator will find himself sighing with relief when the ball, at last, returns safely to the pitcher's glove after its peripatetic travels.

Shelley Perlmutter, first baseperson for Lever Brothers, takes to the air. Woops.

SKIRTS, SHORTS, AND BRITCHES

There were about 40,000 women's amateur teams in the United States ·in 1943 when Philip Knight Wrigley decided to get in the game. Mr. Wrigley was a millionaire. He'd inherited his father's chewing gum company in 1923 when he was twenty-nine and by 1934 he'd become president of his father's baseball club, the Chicago Cubs. By then, the famous Wrigleys had dropped their earliest product, Zeno gum, and were selling the Juicy Fruit, Spearmint, Doublemint that made Chicago famous. By the time the United States entered W.W. II, Wrigley had arranged a contract with the armed forces to provide one stick of gum for every soldier's ration pack. At the height of the war, Wrigley's was producing 600 million sticks of gum a month—7 billion sticks a year—all for consumption by G.I.'s. On the home front, P. K. Wrigley founded the All-American Girls Softball League.

That's where the skirts come in. You see, Mr. Wrigley was a traditional-minded gentleman, and he didn't go for women playing like men. He didn't like these newfangled girls' teams that wore shorts or trousers and carried on their shirts the tempting team names given them by their sponsors—names such as Slapsie Maxie's Curvaceous Cuties, the Num Num Pretzel Girls, Barney Ross's Adorables, and the Dr. Pepper Girls of Miami Beach. No, what Wrigley wanted were respectable names, ladylike costumes, and well-mannered female teams to raise the spirits of war-weary workers.

Wrigley got together with his friends, Paul V. Harper, attorney for the Chicago Cubs, and Branch Rickey, head of the Dodgers, and together they formed a trusteeship for the All-American Girls Softball League. A scout for the Cubs, Jimmy Hamilton, went on the road looking for talent, while a poster artist, Otis Shepard (famed for developing the "Wrigley pixies"), went to work on the uniform.

Shepard decided that what was called for was a simple but elegant flared skirt worn over shorts. The girls were supposed to let their hair grow long and wear ponytails. Put this together with knee socks, short-sleeved blouse with immense lettering on the back, and a sort of modified Sunday school hat with all-round brim, and Mr. Wrigley was presented with a package that looked like a girls' boarding school hockey team costume. Just exactly what he wanted.

The Cub's scout did his job too. He weeded out the bony-looking tomboys, the brawny hitters, uncouth shouters, and other tough cookies, finding teams that not only were hot stuff in the batter's box, but looked pretty trim on the field. Several players came straight from the Bible Institute and Sunday school teams, and as far as scout Hamilton could tell, all were miles above moral re-

Two players from the Grand Rapids (Mich.) Chicks in Wrigley's All-American League. Sophie Kurys slides home and Ruth Lessing makes the tag-out during spring training, 1948.

proach. The pastiche of virtue was formed into four teams—the Rockford (Illinois) Teachers, South Bend (Indiana) Blue Sox, Racine (Wisconsin) Belles, and the Kenosha (Wisconsin) Shamrocks, and they were scheduled for 108 games around the war-busy towns. Their salaries ranged from $125 to $250 a week.

When the girls showed up for spring training at Chicago's Wrigley Field, they got a surprise course in etiquette. Wrigley imported instructors from Helena Rubinstein's Gold Coast Beauty Salon to teach the ladies about make-up, posture, and grooming, which he considered as necessary as pitching, fielding, and hitting. A well-known fashion photographer, Seymour Maurice, made protraits of each player to hang in the lobby of the Wrigley Company. By the first week in June, teams were trained and groomed, and they played an opening double-header at South Bend's Bendix Stadium. In the first night, the Blue Sox got two victories over the Rockford Teachers. The next night, I'm afraid, there was a bit of a row. Evidently two of the players forgot everything they'd learned from Helena, and after a shouting match, went for each other with clenched fists. Fortunately, the umpire separated the ladies before any jaws were broken. But Wrigley winced.

Well, the league flourished for more than ten years, though its beskirted history is now a bit misty. According to Morris Bealle (author of *Softball Story*), Wrigley had a publicity man named Eddie McGuire who kept things moving, recruiting girls from the Chicago Metropolitan Women's Softball League, plus various pro baseball players, to be managers. Many ex-ball players found themselves, in the forties, managing pro women's softball teams. The baseball stars who turned softball managers included Marty McManus, former St. Louis Brown second baseman, Eddie Stumpf of the White Sox, Ralph Boyle of the Brooklyn Dodgers, Johnny Rawlings of the Giants and Pirates, and Bill Wambsganss from the Cleveland Indians.

The Racine Belles, managed by a pro hockey player, won the first League Championship in 1943. The last was won in 1953 by the Fort Wayne (Indiana) Daisies. During the eleven years of women's pro competition, many new teams were added including the Grand Rapids Chicks, the Muskegon Lassies, Peoria Red Wings, and Minneapolis Orphans.

A rival professional league was started in 1944 by the owner of the Chicago Football Cardinals, Charley Bidwill, and Emery Parichy, a woman's-team sponsor who built a softball stadium in Forest Park. In the first year the league included Mr. Bidwill's Blue-birds (he was third-base coach), Parichy's Bloomer Girls, the Rockola Music Maids, Police Sergeant Wragg's Cardinals, the so-called "Chicks"—a team imported from Koch's Furniture Store in Cleveland—and the Brach Candy Kids, sponsored by the Brach Candy Company. The Candy Kids won the pennant, led by a pitcher named Renée Sweet, and I'm not kidding.

During the boom days of women's pro softball in Chicago, many top players were recruited from amateur teams around the country—including Marie Wadlow, Kay Rohrer, Olympia and Frieda Savona, and Dottie Schroeder. These were not sweet young things in short skirts. As amateur players, they wore trousers, ran fast, hit hard, and had plenty of stamina. "Olympia," said one reporter, "runs bases like a man, slides like a man, and catches like a man. If she could spit, she could go with Brooklyn." He added, "Miss Olympia, although built like a football halfback, looks frail compared to Miss Frieda, who handles third base as though born there."

Whether in skirts or britches, the women attracted large crowds in Chicago. A gate of about four thousand was common, and 13,000 came to watch one of the National League games in Bidwill's stadium. Many of these pro players went on to amateur teams after the war ended, and the American and National Women's Softball Leagues folded in 1953.

MIXED SOFTBALL AND MEANINGFUL RELATIONSHIPS

Anyone who plays on a mixed softball team will realize immediately that there are many advantages to be derived from this type of competition. Not only does softball develop mutual respect between the sexes, it can also lead to meaningful relationships between the sexes. (A meaningful relationship, for those who don't know, is whatever you make of it.) For a married person, mixed softball is a way to broaden your social horizons, influence children in a positive manner, extend the family unit, and meet strangers whom you may or may not want to meet. Following are some of the questions that most frequently arise concerning softball and social life:

Q. Can softball change the life of a single person?

A. Yes, definitely. The softball field is an excellent place to meet single people of like-minded interests, as long as those interests are softball, and besides it's much cheaper than Club Méditerranée and all those other swank places where you're (expensively) supposed to develop close friendships with tan people who are single. One particularly fine aspect of mixed teams is that as a single person, you can casually meet a person of the opposite sex sliding through the dust toward your feet. You might offer a helping hand to this person as he or she brushes off the dust. Dust-brushing, in fact, is a great way to get familiar with some-

one. Other ways include: yelling at people; striking them out; hitting grounders to them; and (at closer quarters) having cold drinks with them after the game.

Q. How does softball affect married life?

A. It all depends. If one partner plays softball

Matrimonial Bliss

and the other doesn't, the party that does will have to show a certain regard for the other's feelings. I mean, a wife can't drag her husband to softball games *all* the time just because she happens to be the star pitcher on the team. However, there's no reason why he can't look after the kids once or twice a week while she's doing her innings on the field.

Historically, it must be admitted, the domestic problem has been the reverse. The overly committed male softball player presents his wife with two alternatives:

1. "Good-bye, hon. We're playing Mac-Dougal's. I'll be home at ten."

or

2. "You got the kids ready? Let's go!"

In many cases the wife has allowed the male species to get away with this kind of high-handed behavior. That's fine if she likes keeping track of the kids or watching softball games: she can pack the picnic basket, offspring, husband, and equipment into one vehicle and head *en famille* for the nearest field. If she doesn't like softball, however, it's not so fine, and she may have to put her foot down. What happens when her foot is put down won't be discussed here because the author doesn't like to get involved in family arguments.

The ideal situation is one in which both husband and wife play softball. Then they simply go out and play, and the kids play too, and a couple of hotdogs will suffice for dinner.

Q. Is it safe to introduce children to softball at an early age?

A. Yes, it's not only safe but advisable. Children can begin playing softball at the age of three months or so (using a rubber ball, of course), and many youngsters develop a terrific out-of-the-crib underhand toss before they can walk. By the time a kid is four or five, he should be familiar with most of the fundamentals of softball, and by the age of nine or ten he'll be at the stage that child psychologists call "the point of no return." Loosely defined, this is the point at which a child takes his glove, walks out the door, and leaves his family forever. After a child reaches the point of no return, the only way to get him home is to go down to the softball field and yell parental threats at him. Sometimes even that doesn't work.

Q. Is there any known cure for softball addiction?

A. No. The family of the addicted softballer should realize that he can't help himself. Someone who has played the game since childhood and derived excitement, pleasure, and comfort from his moments on the diamond, is really just a victim of environment and circumstances. By February he'll already be thinking ahead to spring training. Long before the field is groomed and the snows have melted from the earth, the addicted player will be tossing and turning in his sleep as he dreams of unassisted triple plays. You'll find him in the basement, a battered softball in hand, a pile of yellowed news clippings by his side, staring off into space. His attention wanders during cocktail parties or Scrabble games. He seems to forget about that mess in Washington, the energy crisis, the high price of groceries—returning, as if compelled by some mysterious force, to a single unavoidable topic: softball. Whatever happens, the family of the softball addict should be as supportive and understanding as possible. The results are never damaging, and softball may, in fact, help him live a more fulfilled, happy, and satisfying life.

Chapter 6

ODDBALL TEAMS AND STUNT GAMES

THE KING AND HIS COURT

One of the biggest attention getters in the world of softball is also one of the greatest pitchers of all time—and his name is Eddie Feigner.

In 1974 the saga of Eddie Feigner was recounted by Curry Kirkpatrick in *Sports Illustrated,* delivering to the King and His Court a parcel of the fame they so richly deserved. It's a remarkable, screwball story about a man who made his fortune pitching softballs—every which way.

During the spring of 1972, Kirkpatrick encountered the King and His Court at a game show in Dade City, Florida, and tried to find out all there was to know. It turned out to be a lot, since Eddie Feigner is a publicizer and a very sassy talker as well as a super player.

Feigner has a four-man team called "The King and His Court" that will challenge any nine-man team in the country to a game of softball—and the chances are pretty good that

the King will win. For five and a half months out of every year, they crisscross the country, playing to crowds ranging in size from 750 to 15,000. They've played in more than 2,500 cities and town, in cow pastures, on hockey fields and cricket grounds, in penitentiaries, youth camps, hospitals, cemeteries, parking lots, playgrounds, on airplane runways, rifle ranges, stockyards, race tracks, gravel patches, gymnasiums, rodeo arenas, and Astrodomes as well as a few softball diamonds. By the end of 1978 Feigner will have struck out 100,000 men, women, and children. In 7,000 exhibitions, he's already pitched more than 1,500 shutouts, 800 no-hitters, and 200 perfect games.

The key to these landslide victories is Eddie Feigner himself, a healthy man in his fifties with a very slight paunch, a Marine Corps brushcut, an extraordinary throwing arm, and a ball-and-socket joint that is a wonder of anatomical science. His fast ball was clocked at 104 mph, but he says he has thrown faster. He can pitch blindfolded from second base and still strike them out. He once struck out a batter while pitching from center field. He pitches behind his back and between his legs, and sometimes he doesn't pitch at all and the umpire still calls a strike (which I'll explain in a minute). He's got 19 windups, 14 hand deliveries, and 5 speeds—giving him a combined total of 1,300 different pitches in his repertoire.

"My figure-eight windmill with a three-quarter-speed outcurve pitch?" said Feigner to Kirkpatrick. "Forget it. Nobody hits it. I have a whirligig with a crossfire in-drop at three-quarter speed. Forget it, too. School's out. I can't throw hard every day. No one could. But it doesn't matter. If I ever bear down, the teams we play don't have a chance in hell. I still can throw as fast as anybody going. If I could have pitched with three days' rest all my life, I wouldn't have lost ten games yet. My arm never ceases to amaze even me."

Feigner's team combines noise with action for the entertainment of the paying audience. Led by shortstop Gary West, the King and His Court keep up a running patter throughout the game that leaves the spectators neatly tied up in stitches. When the microphone system goes on the blink, as it sometimes does, Feigner can talk to the crowd in a booming voice that's clearly heard in the back row of the bleachers. His quips get laughs— but some of the biggest laughs come when he doesn't pitch at all.

Feigner has a routine where he goes into an elaborate windup, whirling the ball around his head, behind his back, coiling and uncoiling his rubber-boned body like a double-jointed yogi, scrunching into a back-forward and front-backward confusion of arms and legs—and then, finally, firing the ball *behind* him toward the plate. It looks like a pitch, but

Eddie Feigner demonstrates 1/1300th of his repert

in fact this magician of the mound pops the ball into his own glove, and at the same moment the catcher smacks the center of his mitt. Most of the time it happens so fast the umpire calls a strike even though the ball never crosses the plate. The punch line comes when Feigner holds up the ball for the crowd to see, and the umpire must drown his sorrows in a flood of jeers.

Once, however, these shenanigans caused a violent argument between a batter and an umpire. Feigner whipped the ball into his own glove, and per usual the bewildered umpire called a strike.

The batter flew into a rage. The pitch, he howled, was miles high.

Eddie Feigner, still holding the ball in his glove, just laughed.

Sounds like fun, and they make money at it, but The King and His Court follow a grueling schedule, playing more than two hundred games in a season. They do their traveling mostly by car, and Feigner is an expert at scheduling, but the only way to get from town to town is to cover the distance. And some engagements are twenty-two hours apart.

Feigner drives with his precious right arm propped on a pillow, his neck wrapped with toweling, and a bunch of strawberries (when they're in season) by his side. He loves strawberries. Three players travel with him in the van, and occasionally the wives come along.

Eddie Feigner grew up in Walla Walla, Washington, where he learned how to play softball from a friend who was part Cherokee Indian. As a teen-ager, Feigner saw the famed Sioux City Ghosts (a traveling nine-man softball team), and he picked up a few tips from their pitcher. Feigner tried pitching—and by sixteen he was pitching six nights a week in the men's leagues, striking out more batters than they liked. The men of Walla Walla said he could either play the outfield or not play at all. So Eddie Feigner headed for Portland to join the Marines.

Returning to Walla Walla after the war, Feigner played for Kilburg's Grocery in the Green Pea League of the Walla Walla Valley.

In 1946 he pitched against a team from Pendleton, Oregon, and beat them, 33–0. The manager of the Pendleton team insulted Feigner by calling him a "peanut eater," and Feigner responded with a challenge. He said he could beat Pendleton with a four-man team —himself pitching and three others playing catcher, first base, and shortstop.

The following Sunday, the King brought his three-man court into the Walla Walla field and beat Pendleton by a margin of 7–0. News spread fast, and soon the four-man team had challenges from all over the state. They often were asked to play 2-inning exhibition games prior to the regular games of the nine-man teams, but then they found they could keep a crowd happy through an entire 7-inning match. In four years they played nearly 250 games, getting as far away as western Canada. Meanwhile, Feigner had tried just about every kind of profession the Wild West had to offer. He drove trucks, cabs, buses and trolleys, operated cranes, worked docks, played saxophone, kept cost-accounting books, dug ditches, and practiced stand-up comedy. He waited tables, washed dishes, sold cars and vacuum cleaners, installed furnaces, cut asparagus, picked prunes, introduced strippers, pumped gas, sang tenor at funerals, fixed air conditioners, hawked vitamin pills door-to-door, sold burlesque tickets, peddled lumber, wrote sports columns, hammered nails, became a gourmet cook, and served as m.c. for the famous water ski show at Cypress Gardens.

But in 1949 Feigner and the three other whiz kids were jobless, and they decided to do a cross-country tour. They sent out some 3,000 letters to anyone who might conceivably be interested, and got a couple dozen replies—four from Florida. Off they went, booking the return-tour as they traveled across Texas and the South. Their first two games, in Waverly, Florida, earned the team $400. But

Son of Eddie Feigner, J.R. (right), is catcher on the 4-man team. Other players are Gary West at shortstop and Al Jackson on first base.

t was a week until the next game—so they lept on the beach in St. Petersburg and bided heir time. The tour seemed to be a bust. They earned the Amateur Softball Association had orbidden any of its member teams to play against the King and His Court.

Only one more game was scheduled—at Al Lang Field near St. Petersburg. On the way to the field, Feigner got stuck in a traffic jam. He thought it was bingo night, but, in fact, the crowd was waiting to see the famous King and His Court from Walla Walla play a local team. There were 2,400 fans there that night.

Among the spectators was a promoter for the Canadian National Exhibition. He invited Feigner to come north and play the number-one softball team in North America, the Tip Top Tailors. The King said, "Sure," and on September 8, in front of overflow crowds, the four-man team held the Tip Top Tailors to a 0–0 draw in a 9-inning game. The King and His Court were home free.

Today, Eddie Feigner is a legendary figure to softball players everywhere. His name crops up over and over again. Now he's playing against a second generation of soft-ballers (and still winning), and to many he's a reminder of the great days of fast pitch. People who saw him play never forget it. Hotshot sluggers shake their heads, remembering how he struck them out pitching from second base. If you got a hit off Feigner, you're a mentiona-ble local celebrity.

While admittedly a stunt pitcher, Feigner and his three fielders play nine-man teams that are out to beat him. Even if he's traveled six-teen hours the night before, with two hours' sleep in an over-air-conditioned motel room and fifteen minutes warmup before a triple-header, he still gives it everything he's got. In-cluding his figure-eight windmill with a three-quarter-speed outcurve.

THE QUEEN AND HER COURT

It had to happen. If there could be an Eddie Feigner and his four-man team, then there had to be somebody and her four-*woman* team. That somebody was Rosie Beaird.

It was Dad's idea, however. Royal Beaird (pronounced Baird) is all-round coach, man-ager, rooter, and promoter, with a powerful streak of Metro-Goldwyn-Mayer in his char-acter. In 1964 this softball addict founded the "Kids Klub" in Rolling Hills, California, and then taught his eleven-year-old daughter, Rosie, how to pitch. She pitched fine, and pretty soon there wasn't a team that could stand up to her, but then Royal had the prob-lem of finding a catcher who could work with her. When Rosie's sister Eileen reached the age of eight, Royal put her in.

Soon there was Karen Beaird to play first base, and a high school chum of Rosie's named Debby Bevers was asked to play third.

Rosie Black delivers strike-out pitch between her legs during performance of The Queen and Her Maids.

In 1965 Royal sent the four girls on a summer tour of Texas and Utah, and the Queen and Her Maids (as the team was first called) drew record crowds in fourteen cities. That was the beginning of the traveling show.

By 1976 Rosie Beaird had become Rosie Black. The Queen had also struck out 24,063 batters, pitched 362 shutouts, 257 no-hitters, and 104 perfect games. The team added pregame juggling to its act, and a talented shortstop named Lotta Chatter provided a comedy routine on the field. They were covering about 40,000 miles a year with their traveling show, sometimes playing for crowds of 30,000 or more. The team is paid on a guaranteed basis, but games are usually for benefits, and some of the gate goes toward charity.

Rosie has developed the gyrotechnics of an Eddie Feigner—pitching between her legs, behind her back, from second base, and blindfolded—and the four so-called "gals" have made mice out of many nine-man teams.

Since the early days of the Maids, Papa has kept the girls on a rigid health program. They run more than a mile every day, swim and do water calisthenics, and their regime forbids such unsavory items as cigarettes, alcohol, and drugs. According to the Queen's souvenir booklet, "Rosie and her husband, Darrell, enjoy attending church, worshipping the Lord, and having fellowship with their Christian friends." Their summer schedule is hectic, and Rosie sometimes pitches ten games a week, but she doesn't seem to mind. In fact, she calls it "a dream job."

Rosie, it should be added, is universally acknowledged to be a beautiful person, and she can also throw the ball at about 90 mph. These combined virtues have landed her on a number of television programs. On Dick Cavett she struck out two of the New York Mets —Art Shamsky and Ed Kranepool—though Ron Swoboda got a weak grounder off her. Willie Mays managed to hit a high fly in front of Merv Griffin's audience, but he later admitted she was one of the best pitchers he'd ever faced.

The Queen's troupe can do an untold amount of damage to the male ego in a single game. Occasionally they'll let a male pitcher do his stuff for a few innings—then, bam, they come back with fifteen runs in a row. Their batting is as solid as their fielding and pitching. Royal Beaird, on the side lines, usually calls the pitches, and Rosie serves them up, while the local batting champ begins to look like a chump. Show-person to the last, Royal has a standing offer of $5.00 to anyone who can hit the ball fair off Rosie's pitch in a pregame exhibition. Occasionally, they do. But then Royal jumps in.

"Hey, you're pretty good," he says. "Tell you what, you hit another one, I'll double your money. Double or nothing!"

This dare puts the batter on the spot. Does he take his five bucks and walk away— admitting that he doesn't have a chance at the second pitch? Or does he accept the offer? Most accept.

"But they don't hit me a second time," says Rosie.

SOFTBALL OVER THE HILL

Early in November, two teams troop onto the field at North Shore Park in St. Petersburg, Florida. The Kids wear blue caps and the Kubs wear red caps, but otherwise their uniforms are identical—white shirts, sweaters, long duck trousers, bow ties, and sneakers.

The leader, flag bearer, and umpire gather at home plate, with the Kids in a line between third and home, and the Kubs, between first and home. Leader and flag bearer march out across the pitcher's mound, stopping short of home plate. Kids and Kubs swing toward the center, coming to a halt in a double line. They face front, toward home plate, and sing "America the Beautiful" with the audience joining in. Then they give the club cheer:

What's the matter with 75?
We're the boys who're all alive.
Hi ho, Let's go.
Rah, rah, rah, 75.

The flag bearer and leader rejoin the umpires at home plate, and the teams march double-file through the pitcher's box to home, where they salute the flag and are formally dismissed by the leader.

This formal opening precedes every game of St. Petersburg's Three-Quarter Century Club, an exclusive softball league for young men seventy-five years or older.

The Club was founded in 1930 when Evelyn Barton Rittenhouse, a retired actress, was looking around for activities for her Three-Quarter Century Society in St. Pete. The old boys were pretty well occupied with bridge and poker and flirting in the evenings, but it was obvious they needed something to fill their sunny days in Florida. When Mrs. Rittenhouse observed a venerable team playing in Wisconsin, she decided to transport the idea southward and sell it to the St. Petersburg Chamber of Commerce.

When she approached the C of C, however, the members weren't overwhelmed. "What happens if someone drops dead?" they asked. Mrs. Rittenhouse adopted a try-it-and-see policy, got together eighteen men, and after a few minutes of practice, they all went down to City Hall to have their pictures taken. The Three-Quarter Century Club was officially born.

The Kids and Kubs play three days a week, and they're in good shape all season. (A "season" in this case, extends from November through April—the vacation months in Florida.) In the early games, they had a rule that the fielders had to walk after ground balls, and the runners had to walk around the bases. The rule didn't last long. One outfielder, going for a fly ball, started walking faster and faster, and by the time he snagged the ball, he was moving at a speed that everyone considered a fast run. He was thrown out of the game, but you can't hold back progress. The ice was bro-

The 1976–77 Kids and Kubs of the Three-Quarter Century Club, who bill themselves as "the ninth wonder of this modern age." Eldest in the photo are James Waldie (91) and Fred Broadwell (92)—second and third from left in the first row.

ken again by an argumentative and unreasonable batter who said, "Hell, if I hit the ball, I'm gonna run for all I'm worth." He hit, he ran, and the rule went to blazes.

The men come from all over the United States—only a few live in St. Petersburg—and players have to try out for the team and be approved by a majority of players. Once on, however, the players maintain an admirable barter system that keeps the teams even. When the Kubs lead by three games, their captain gets to choose one player from the Kids—in exchange for one of the Kubs' poorer players. In this way, neither of the teams gets much more than a three-game lead before things even up again. But there's spirited competition for high batting records, home-run records, and pitching triumphs.

In 1975–76 the top pitcher was Albert Kuster, age 78, a former machine operator for the New York Highway Department. In his fifth year with the Kids and Kubs, he won 16 and lost 13. Award for the best batting average went to Edward Stauffer, age 79, and the top home-run sluggers were Frank Martin, 77, from the Kubs, and Everett Chapman, 76, of the Kids. Stauffer is one of the few Three-Quarter Century Clubbers who played pro ball; later he became general manager for the Major Electric Appliance Company in Pittsburgh. Martin was a railroad clerk and yardmaster for the B & O and Central Railroads for forty-five years, and Chapman was a machinist with General Dynamics for thirty-two years. The combined ages of the two squads, in 1976, amounted to 2,479 years.

Games attract audiences of 2–3,000 plus stray dogs and sea gulls and an occasional big league ball player who takes a break from spring training to cheer the grandpas. The story is told of a cantankerous member of the Kubs who was playing outfield during a practice game, when he spotted two uniformed ballplayers crossing the outfield. The old Kub was annoyed at having the interlopers in his territory.

"You youngsters better look sharp or you'll get hurt!" he shouted. Babe Ruth and Lou Gehrig skedaddled.

Other guests to the field have included Russ Meyer, Stan Musial, Bob Feller, and Yogi Berra. Connie Mack and Casey Stengel were made honorary members.

Many past team members of the Kids and

Kids meet Kubs, 1949. The Kids grabbed the championship that year by a margin of 11–8.

Kubs achieved fame—or notoriety—in their own time and their own way. Historians protect the name of the outfielder who should have worn suspenders, but didn't. We know from records that he must have been shaped something like a kewpie doll, and his girth must have been larger than any belt could encompass. On one occasion he raced after a fly ball, got under it, reached up and snagged it just as his pants fell to the earth. His knees, said spectators, were knobby.

Then there's the one about the home-run hitter who poked a high fly over the left-field fence to win the game for the Kubs. To the cheers of the crowd, he began a leisurely trot around the bases. He got past third and was well on his way toward home when he suddenly stopped, turned around, and ran back to third. To the astonishment of the fans, he dropped to his hands and knees and began searching in the dust.

"What the hell are you doing?" asked the Kids' third baseman.

The aged Kub looked up and gave the Kid a toothless smile.

"I lost my teesh," he replied.

And of course there's a story about a preacher. It was in the final innings of a close game, and a retired minister came up to bat. The man of the cloth said a quick prayer and belted a grounder to right field for an easy double. The second baseman, however, didn't get out of the way soon enough, and the minister came in full steam, knocking the player flat. The second baseman got up swinging, the minister swung back, and in a minute they were going at it fast and furious.

"Hold it!" cried the runner suddenly.

"What's the matter, you S-O-B?" yelled the second baseman.

The runner held up his hands as a sign of peace.

"Sorry, brother," he said, "I forgot I was a preacher once."

And that ended the fight.

The average age of the Kids and Kubs is 86, and some players have stayed in the field while they were well up in their nineties. One elderly lady asked a player who had just hit a home run and raced around the bases, "Aren't you afraid of straining your heart playing ball?" He replied, "Madam, people with weak hearts don't live to reach my age."

Most famous of the century-pushers was Charlie Eldridge. He played until he was 102, but then he had to quit. You see, he'd been shot in the arm during the Civil War, and the Minié ball lodged in his bicep started to "pain a bit."

And they're still talking about John

Charles Eldridge (102), captain of the Kubs in 1933, holds the ball with Babe Ruth. The Babe was a frequent visitor to the field and sometimes served as base umpire.

Maloney, the tall, ambling, venerable right-hander who pitched twenty-one years and eight hundred games for the Kids and Kubs. When he first joined the team in 1952, he practiced every day except Sunday, perfecting a kind of pitch that tied the seventy-fivers in knots. "They have always told me no one can really hit homers off me," he told a reporter. "I put this kind of spin on the ball that makes it tough to hit. I don't think anyone ever hit the ball square."

On a clear, cool day in April 1973 John Maloney threw his last pitch in an exhibition game. He was 96 years old, and he could hardly see the ball any more.

"I'm going blind," he said. "My eyesight is all shot. I can't see any more. I have to give it up."

On April 30, he flew home to stay with his sixty-seven-year-old daughter in Madison, New Jersey. People had told him he would pitch until he was a hundred, but he said, "I don't think I'll be back.

John Maloney, the world's oldest pitcher, never returned to the mound. He died in January 1974, in Madison, New Jersey.

THE SHOW-OFFS

"I wouldn't want to belong to any club that would have me as a member," says Woody Allen. But he never objected to belonging to his own softball club—did he? No. In fact, Woody Allen is known around the Broadway Show League as being the founding father of Schlissel's Schleppers, once a very hot team. He's also known as a very tough ballplayer. And not the only one.

Al Pacino plays softball. George C. Scott plays softball. Colleen Dewhurst, Paul Newman, Walter Matthau, and Ben Gazzara have all played softball at one time or another during their otherwise distinguished careers. To name-drop only a few. And what's the purpose of this name-dropping? Oh, to show they're human. To prove they can strike out just like you and me.

It should bring them down a peg or two, behaving like that on Thursday afternoons in Central Park. But it doesn't. In fact, they usually feel better. Healthier, more alive, possibly (who knows) even more starlike. For a place to show off, there is nothing, repeat nothing, in the world like that softball diamond. When the showbiz people get tired of the stage, this is where they come to show off.

Some actors and actresses get very serious about softball. Ben Gazzara once broke his arm during a game, and the accident cost him a $5,000-a-week movie contract. Actor Tony LoBianco flew in from Hollywood, leaving the set of the TV show "Get Smart" to pitch in the play-offs. His team won. Hector Elizondo, who played opposite George C. Scott in the Broadway production of *Sly Fox,* said, "One should never forget the art of playing. I enjoy a good game and don't worry about the outcome. This is a great meeting place—an outdoor saloon and pub."

That probably sums up the feelings of most of the talented people who play in the Broadway Show League. When the league was founded by John Effrat in 1955, it was under the auspices of the Actors' Fund of America and its purpose was "to provide an opportunity for companies playing on Broadway to engage in a healthful outdoor physical activity." When Effrat died in 1965, a New York attorney, Michael Frankfurt, took over as commissioner, and from him the League passed on (three years later) to Fran Lewin, a Broadway fan who has ruled the diamonds like a strict godmother.

In 1972 the foundations of the show league were shaken by a dispute between good-timers and hotshots within the league. It seems that several teams had been recruiting "ringers" to play in the Show League—that is, semi-pro ballplayers who wore spikes, pitched fast, and played for keeps. The leader of this play-tough movement was Jim Jensen, a newscaster who was pitcher on the WCBS team. For several years, Jensen's team had been improving steadily as he recruited more and more ringers from outside the Show League. By 1971 he had one of the best squads in the league, but the just-for-fun players resented having to play against a bunch of WCBS hotshots who looked like pros. Finally, it came to a showdown between Jim Jensen and Fran Lewin.

Jim Jensen, pitcher for WCBS All-Stars, warming up for a Tuesday-afternoon game in Central Park.

On opening day, April 20, 1972, Fran confronted Jim and announced that no ringers would be allowed in the League during the forthcoming season. Jim said he'd use whatever talent he could find. A team of cameramen from WCBS recorded the historic confrontation, and the scene was aired on the evening news program.

"Fran wants the game to be like fat men versus skinny men at a church picnic," Jensen told a reporter from the *New Yorker.* "My pleasure comes in playing hard, playing clear, playing professional, and playing to win. Whatever you're doing, do it well—that's what the kick is."

That confrontation led to the start of a new league. The following season, Jensen and a number of other teams formed a new association called the Show Business League that played on Tuesday afternoons instead of on Thursdays. Today this League includes a variety of hotshot teams from broadcast stations, bars, restaurants, and hangouts around the city. Jensen's WCBS All-Stars has former professional baseball players, one or two ringers from the WCBS studio, and a number of TV celebrities.

In addition to their Central Park performances, the All-Stars have been playing benefit games since 1971, and have made about $300,000 for various charities. On Thursdays (after Jensen's 6 o'clock broadcast), and on Sunday afternoons, the All-Stars travel to nearby towns in New York, New Jersey, and Connecticut, where they face challengers from the local teams. Jensen, steely-haired and square-jawed, is still the pitcher and the main attraction for autograph hunters. At the age of fifty, Jensen admits that he still gets a thrill from the crowd that watches him play and cheers his pitching. "It may be extended adolescence," he admits. "But who cares?"

After the ringers went away, the Broad-way Show League regathered its forces, signed up new teams and repeated its commitment to softball-for-fun. Fran Lewin submitted her tearful resignation to the Actors' Fund, but they wouldn't let her go. Gray-haired, chatty, she is a dynamo of a commissioner. On Thursday afternoons, she pedals around on a mini-bike, visiting each of the five diamonds on the Heckscher Playing Field in Central Park, making sure every Broadway Show League team has its allocation of softballs, pays its umpires, and doesn't use ringers. The Show League games are riddled with errors, and most of the players don't give a hoot. But a few actors admit that they sometimes get carried away and start playing a bit rougher than they intended—especially near the end of the season, when the championship hangs in balance.

Long-running shows obviously have a better chance of developing the talents of their players. Occasionally, some teams have to fold in midseason if the show closes down, but players are allowed to continue on Thursday afternoons even if the theater is dark Thursday night.

The first winner was *Silk Stockings* in 1955 followed by *Mr. Wonderful* and *Bells Are Ringing. My Fair Lady* cleaned up three years in a row, but later got stiff competition from the staff of Circle-in-the-Square Theatre and the cast of *A Thousand Clowns.* Other winners include the New York Shakespeare Festival and cast of *The Wiz.* In 1972 the Most Valuable Player Award of the year went to Sygna Joy of *Two Gentlemen of Verona.*

Because these softballers are emotional artist types, there are storms that brew and occasionally break on the playing field. Woody Allen takes softball in dead earnestness, and says, "I'm crushed when there are errors. I want to win badly, and I play my heart out."

George C. Scott is well known for his explosive temper on the field. He stands about

Woody Allen and Tony Roberts of Schlissel's Schleppers alongside Lee Meredith, pinch hitter. The occasion, a benefit performance for patients at a VA hospital.

six feet, weighs around 200 pounds, and when he's enraged he's like a mad bull. During one Broadway show, he was pitching for a team that was playing a crucial end-of-the-season game. The umpire made a call which Scott disagreed with, strongly. He went roaring toward the plate like a 200-pound locomotive. The 5'7" fifty-nine-year-old umpire backed away, whipped off his mask, and tossed it in Mr. Scott's million-dollar face.

"I don't know what got him so upset," Scott recalled at a later and calmer time. "All I did was call him a dirty rotten so-and-so."

POLITICAL SOFTBALL

Politicians, as we all know, will do anything to get attention, and the President of the United States, Jimmy Carter, who thinks he can pitch, is no exception. Carter's softball springs from home-town Georgian roots, where he played in the Plains Church League. His motive for becoming President was to recruit the obviously more talented, trim and physically fit members of the Secret Service who—you will notice—always play on Jimmy's side. That way Jimmy wins. And anyone who watched him smile after the election knows that Jimmy likes to win.

Without his Secret Service men, Jimmy would be in big trouble on the softball diamond. The fact that Jimmy needs his Secret Service is clearly borne out by the events of August 8, 1976. That day, in the middle of the election campaign, the little town of Plains, Georgia (pop. 683) was packed with a coterie of journalists, campaigners and hangers-around, and Saturday night there was a big fish fry in an empty peanut warehouse owned by the Carters. Ralph Nader spent the night, and although he wasn't endorsing any politicians, he declared that Jimmy Carter's policies were "admirable" and a "breath of fresh air."

Sunday morning, there was a softball game. The Secret Service men were all around the field in their morbid black cars, but they decided not to take part in the game. So it was a "choose-up" game among the visiting journalists and Plains residents, with Billy Carter pitching for the opposing side. Ralph Nader was umpire, and he insisted that all players fasten their belts and protect the environment by not spitting tobacco juice on the field.

For the first time in weeks, the score went against the candidate. Billy Carter's team was leading, 10–3, with 2 out in the bottom of the ninth, when a sudden explosion split the air.

"Get those vehicles onto the field," barked a Secret Service man, and the guard patrol raced in from the periphery of the field. Jimmy just stood and stared at the cloud of black smoke rising over Billy's service station, while his brother raced the two hundred yards to his property in about 10.3.

Well, evidently there had been a short circuit in the soda machine, causing an explosion when some gas fumes escaped. A 3,000-gallon tanker truck standing in the station was safely moved out of the way, and no one was injured except a couple of kids from the Alabama Congregational Church—who got slight burns. But that ended the game and saved Jimmy from the embarrassment of defeat.

Remember Watergate? Well, it had long been a tradition for Senator Sam Ervin's Judiciary Subcommittee to play the White House staff, and being very sportspersonlike, they went right ahead with the game in the midst of

The presidential style. Catcher is Jody Powell, with Ralph Nader as ump.

the Watergate crisis. On June 2, 1973, Sam's Sluggers beat the White House Assistants in a close game, 10–9, which Ervin was unable to attend. (It was a busy time for the Ervin panel, as it was about to investigate the burglary of Ellsberg's psychiatrist's office. Ehrlichman had just placed the blame for the cover-up on Dean, and Kalmbach was getting ready to testify, but out in Potomac Park near the tidal basin, all was harmonious on the softball diamond.)

Sam's Sluggers consisted of twenty team members, most of them wearing shorts and dark blue T-shirts, and the White House team was made up of a variety of assistants and assistants-to-assistants. Hence their name, the Assistants. It was 86 degrees, and the gnats were terrible. The coach for Sam's Sluggers was Bill Pursley, chief council for the Revision and Codification Subcommittee of the Judiciary Committee, who judiciously gave everyone his or her chance on the field.

The White House hit a lot of fly balls into the press section, but the Assistants denied that this had anything to do with a vendetta against the press. The New York *Times* carried a complete story of the game, and for a moment there, it looked like the nation's problems might be solved on the ball field. But the next day, politics were back to normal.

Another political situation fraught with tension was the meeting, on August 19, 1976, between a team from the office of Mayor Beame of New York and the State Emergency Financial Control Board, in a softball game at Riverside Park and 103rd Street. It was the height of New York City's financial crisis, with daily meetings taking place in City Hall to determine who should have control over the city's finances—the city or the state. Called in as auditors and advisors, the SEFCB had been pitching some very bad news in the direction of the mayor's office during the past weeks.

Beame's Team

As it turned out, Beame's team won by a landslide, 26–9, but the figures were immediately disputed by Stephen Berger, executive director of the Control Board. Wearing a bright orange T-shirt labeled, "It's not my job," Mr. Berger noted that the Board had the prerogative to review and approve Beame Administration figures, and he concluded, "We won, 6–0."

The reason, he explained, was that the city started with a 3-run deficit. When it earned its first 3 runs, Beame's team was back to 0, and any runs scored over that had to go in an emergency contingency reserve as directed by the SEFCB. The Board's decision was spelled out in a report contained in a "pumpkin-colored folder"—the kind used to hold the city's audits.

A New York *Times* reporter, sensing an optimistic trend for the city, was quick to interview the mayor's players. Lou Venech, a young member of the staff, commented,

"We're tough because we're lean. We're the ones who have had the layoffs." When the mayor's squad was 17 runs up, one of his aides had the heart to comment, "Things have never looked so good for the city."

The only conflict was reported after Aeric Kaston, a twenty-three-year-old mayoral assistant, caught what looked like a line drive close to the ground. He made the throw to second base for the force-out. A member of the State Board, however, insisted it wasn't a line drive Kaston had caught, but a low grounder. In an eyeball-to-eyeball confrontation, the state and city came to a compromise and decided it was 1 out instead of 2 against the State.

NINE OLD MEN

Rarely has there been such a mingling of the literary, scholarly, theatrical, and political with the high art of softball. Never, in the history of America, have such cultural giants made such fools of themselves. Never has there been such a mistreatment of the game since the unforgettable days of the Nine Old Men.

The Nine Old Men was a crazed sort of recreational softball team founded in the Thirties by Lowell Thomas, Ted Shane, and a number of other well-known personages who lived in the area of Pawling, New York, plus many stray luminaries who showed up for the weekend games. In those days the tournaments were major local events—attended by some 2,500 people who came to watch the mental giants of their time make spectacles of themselves.

Many famous men played on the Pawling team—or faced the Nine Old Men in grueling competition. Team members, at various times, included Casey Hogate, better known as "Flash," publisher of the *Wall Street Journal*,

Secretary of the Treasury Henry Morgenthau (second base), Captain Frank Hawks (record holder for the first non-stop transcontinental airplane flight), Gene Tunney (former boxer), cartoonist Paul Webb, better known as "Slugger," Dale Carnegie (famed for *How to Win Friends and Influence People*), and Congressman Hamilton Fish. Also drifting on and off the team were a bevy of businessmen, politicians, adventurers, and literary men who played whenever they were in town, and could get away from their wives.

Every year the Nine Old Men faced a number of formidable opponents, including a White House team made up of newspaper correspondents, Secret Service men, secretaries, and cabinet members, with Franklin D. Roosevelt as manager. At the other end of the political spectrum were the Oystervelts of Roose Bay, better known as the Bad Oysters, headed by Colonel Ted Roosevelt. This crowd included Rube Goldberg, Merlin H. Aylesworth (publisher of the *World-Telegram*), Truman Talley (head of Movietown Newsreels), Babe

The Nine Old Men, numbering 14. (Couldn't they count? Or are there impostors here?) The fellow with the badges is Les Cramer, better known as "Napoleon." At far right, Lowell Thomas and his infallible assistant and pitcher, Prosper Buranelli.

Ruth ("not very expert at hitting"), magician John Mulholland, Bernard Gimbel of department store fame, and Robert Ripley, believe it or not.

There was also a formidable gang of literary giants hailing from eastern Connecticut, called "George Bye's Nutmegs." George Bye was a literary agent, and his powerful nine included Harold Ross, editor of the *New Yorker,* Richard L. Simon (of Simon and Schuster) as well as the sportswriter Quentin Reynolds. Their team cheer was a disaster, metric-wise, and it went like this:

Let's lose, let's lose, let's lose, let's lose,
If losing will mean to our opponents good news.

A number of *ad hoc* teams were assembled, from time to time, to face the terrifying threat of the Nine Old Men. Challengers included the New York Ad Club, the Fox Movietone News, Saints and Sinners Lunch Club, Bob Ripley's "Believe It or Nuts," the New York Artists and Models Guild, and the Explorers Club of New York.

In later years, Lowell Thomas and Ted

Shane wrote of their escapades and disasters in a book called, *Softball: So What?* wherein is described the early, slightly absurd history of this Pawling softball movement. It all began in 1933 as a way to distract both the Haves and the Have-nots from the overhanging gloom of the Depression. The Haves, according to the authors, were the prosperous merchants of Pawling, and the Have-nots were residents of the historic village of Quaker Hill. Since most of the players in Quaker Hill owed a consid-

erable amount of money to the merchants, the residents were called the Debtors, and the merchants the Creditors. A game was scheduled, and the Doughty Debtors met the Crushing Creditors on a blazing hot day in the middle of the summer. Midway through the game, there was some sort of controversy over a close play, and suddenly everyone remembered that the people from Quaker Hill didn't get along with the people from Pawling. An argument ensued of such ferocious intensity

Franklin D. Roosevelt, manager of the White House gang, with Lowell Thomas of the Nine Old Men, 1937. Their teams clashed on the site of the Old Quaker Hill Golf Club in Pawling.

that, by the end of the day, the two teams had agreed that they would never play against each other again. Instead, they would play together.

Thus was born the Debtors and Creditors, better known as the Nine Old Men (a reference to U. S. Supreme Court justices). As reported by Lowell and Shane, the aggregate weight of the N.O.M. was in the range of 2,000 pounds. Number of muscles: four. Number of strained muscles: four.

Meanwhile, thirty miles away in Hyde Park, President Franklin D. Roosevelt and the "White House Menage" were suffering in the blazing heat of August, just waiting to get out and play some softball. So Lowell Thomas and Casey (*Wall Street Journal*) Hogate issued an invitation to the Executive Branch to meet the Pawling terrorists on their own field. F.D.R. arrived in his open limousine and managed his team from a throne of buffed leather.

Of course, this was a highly charged political forum as well as a rugged softball game, and F.D.R. seized the opportunity to comment on the base-running of the *Wall Street Journal* editor. Casey, though not related to the kid in the poem, was quite a slugger. He was also quite round and heavy. In fact, he was described as "one of the softball whales," and his total weight was estimated to be somewhere near a seventh of a ton. When Casey dropped by the limousine to talk with the press, Roosevelt commented:

"They tell me, Mr. Hogate, that you have to make a home run to get to first base!"

The remark, I'm afraid, must have struck a sore spot. The Wall Street editor never did have anything complimentary to say about the New Deal.

Secretary of the Treasury Morgenthau also got a wicked backlash from opposing players who complained about taxes, deplored an ill-managed economy, and in general used every possible insult to get him riled at the plate.

In-jokes proliferated, *ad nauseam*. It was said that Thomas Dewey, later to be governor of Connecticut, was so busy cleaning up crime that he never let a man steal a base. Players joked about John Mulholland, the magician, who could make the ball vanish—but had trouble catching it.

"The Nine Old Men," wrote Thomas and Shane, "are smooth-functioning, age-resisting, rustproof, softball organisms which defy the laws of gravity, have been known to stand up an entire game, and manage to hold their own on any softball field where their opponents do not exceed them by two inches in circumference. Though many of them have let their bodies go to their heads, they are all perfect sportsmen. None is swelled-headed about his softball. Why should he be?"

Despite their overwhelming modesty, however, particular heroes had their peculiar moments of glory. On June 19, 1938, in a game with Teddy Roosevelt's Oysters in Pawling, cartoonist Rube Goldberg made history by pitching five innings with a cigar in his mouth. Not only that, he managed to give up 32 hits, allowing the Nine Old Men to score 19.

An old favorite at third base was F. Chase Taylor, a retired broker, better known as Colonel Lemuel Q. Stoopnagle. Apparently, Stoopnagle's girth was as huge and intimidating as his sense of humor. He had a consistent .005 batting average, wore spats, and was sole owner of a patent for the curved bat—to hit a curve-ball pitch.

Favorite pitcher was Prosper (hit-'em-a-mile) Buranelli, well known for never having struck out a single man. He was under five feet tall, had twelve children, and firmly believed that softball was a silly game. His playing was a testament to this belief. One of his shrewdest tactics was to bounce the ball in front of the

Colonel Lemuel Q. Stoopnagle, carrying a mere fraction of his extensive bat collection. Would you buy a used bat from this man?

batter, in hopes that the slugger would take a swing.

Another, much larger example of human dynamism, Heywood Broun, earned everyone's appreciation by getting his wife to run bases for him. Not only did she get to first base minutes before Broun would have arrived, she was also much more fun to watch.

But the player who undoubtedly took the most abuse, among all the Nine Old Men, was the outfielder Dale Carnegie. Carnegie made his mistake before he even got on the team, by writing *How to Win Friends and Influence People*. It became obvious to his teammates, who took pity on him, that Dale Carnegie had

no friends and was absolutely incapable of influencing anyone. Thomas and Shane described him as "a natty eye-glassed business man, absolutely timid and lonely, standing off by himself at the edge of a crowd, utterly disregarded by everyone." It was obvious that Mr. Carnegie had turned to softball only because his book had failed so miserably to help win him companions.

Carnegie not only played atrociously, he also had no sense of decorum. In the outfield he wore a long overcoat and a soft crushed hat. There were so many objections to this outrageous attire that the Nine Old Men almost broke up over the issue of Carnegie's

The Great Pawling Softball Disaster, presented by the intellectual giants of a bygone era.

overcoat. In the Spring of 1938 Colonel Stoopnagle and cartoonist Paul Webb refused to sign a contract with the Nine Old Men—chiefly because of Dale Carnegie's overcoat. Stoopnagle said flat out, he would not play if Carnegie insisted on wearing his overcoat. Lowell Thomas said he had seen D.C. play *with* and *without* the overcoat, and he was a much better player with the overcoat, so it should be left in. When it came down to the wire, however, it turned out that Stoopnagle really wanted the overcoat to play without Dale Carnegie.

In the end Carnegie played in pleated pants, suspenders, and a panama hat, but apparently this outfit didn't win him any friends either. He still couldn't catch a ball.

Eventually the Nine Old Men became older and wiser, and they contributed their good (and bad) advice for future softballers. The team captains gathered numerous suggestions on how not to pitch, how not to hit, and how not to play the field. For instance, to recover from a batting slump, Stoopnagle tried using two bats instead of one—but a sharp-witted pitcher started throwing him two balls instead of one. Comedian Lew Lehr used a slightly different approach: while at bat, he'd lie down on the base, concealing it from the pitcher, and get a base on balls. Paul Webb nurtured himself out of batting slumps by going on a diet of Wheaties dunked in beer. Prosper Buranelli, a self-proclaimed "Cripple-A-Softball" pitcher, recommended a low inside toss that would lie well under the paunch of the batter. That way, the batter couldn't touch it. For the catcher, Lew Lehr suggested that he never throw to second base, because any runner who got that far deserved to stay there.

The fate of the Nine Old Men is not entirely known, though of course many of the players survived softball to become legends in their own time. Returning to the green fields of Pawling, one can, perhaps, hear the echo of Hogate, Stoopnagle, and Morgenthau shouting to their teammates, and the thunder of these overweights as they make their way around the bases. There, for a decade, the nation's leaders gathered in harmony, to run like elephants and to swing like woodsmen. Perhaps it was there on the softball field they gathered new energy, new ideas, and new courage to help guide the course of a nation. And you wonder why we're in trouble?

Chapter 7

I'LL FLIP YOU FOR SHIFTY

HALL OF FAME

One of the pleasures of growing up in America is buying baseball cards with your bubble gum. One skinny little flat piece of bubble gum is all you get, colored pink, tasting like flavored chalk, with that crusty sort of texture that is transformed into a formless glob only after you've used horrendous amounts of naturally produced saliva. But the real prize is the set of baseball cards that comes with the gum. There's a picture of a player on the front of each card, his team name inscribed on a banner, and the player's signature in bold scrawl across his chest or thigh. Turn it over, and you have the whole story. Height, weight, birth date, home town, and myriad statistics, including G's, AB's, R's, H's, 2B's, 3B's, HR's, RBI's, and AVG's for each year he played. And off to one side, in a box with a semicomical sort of drawing, is a sliver of nonsensical information that has nothing whatever to do with the player.

Now the card itself is of little or no intrinsic value. It's just a piece of cardboard. But *which* piece of cardboard do you own—that's the question. Do you have a Mickey Mantle, 1968? I'll flip you for a 1967 Whitey Ford, 'cause I've got two? What if I throw in a Sandy Koufax, 1965? He pitched a perfect game that year. Okay, two for one, I'll flip you, here goes . . .

I've heard several versions of how to flip for baseball cards. It seems to depend on what part of the country you're from, and what was your neighborhood tradition. The way we did it, you took the card between thumb and two middle fingers, holding along the edges, see, and snapped it sharply so it flew through the air and came to rest near a wall. Then the other guy flipped, and if his card came closer to the wall, he got both of them. I've also heard of versions where one card has to cover the other, but I never played that way.

Anyhow, I don't know whether you noticed or not, but among all those baseball cards, there wasn't a single, no, not one single *softball* card. How do you like that? Softball, with the greatest pitchers in the nation, and some of the sharpest fielding and highest batting AVG's anywhere, and what attention do these players get from the bubble gum company? Nothing. Hundreds of millions of people going to softball games, tens of millions playing the game, and for some incomprehensible reason no one sees fit to publish softball cards. It's outrageous!·

Well, enough griping about the situation. This chapter is a small attempt to correct that discrepancy as much as possible. On the following pages you will find some of the greatest softball players of the century, all members of the Amateur Softball Association's Hall of Fame. Since this is a novelty in the world of bubble gum, we won't include all the statistics for these greats—just some background on a few of them, to show what they're doing in the Hall of Fame. Also included are a few car-

toons and little-known facts about softball, which you'll probably want to memorize.

Don't get the idea this collection is complete. There are lots of great softball players around today who aren't in the Hall of Fame, but should be, and others—like yourself—you will want to nominate. This is just a starting point for your collection. If you're really serious about it, you can cut out the players' pictures, stick them to pieces of cardboard, and you're ready to compete. I'll flip you for Shifty.

HAROLD GEARS
Nickname: "Shifty"
Pitcher
Home: Rochester, New York
Elected Hall of Fame: 1957

Background: Could pitch with both hands. Started in 1922, age 14, with the Silver Stars.

ASA Hall of Fame

Harold "Shifty" Gears

Last played with Redeemer Church in 1951, at 43. In 40 years as recreation counselor with Eastman Kodak Company, he sponsored outstanding junior softball program.

Record: In 1931 pitched 10 games in 10 days, winning Canadian Crown of the International League in the first 5, then capturing the International Championship from the American champs, the Goldies. Lifetime record: 866 victories and 115 defeats. Played 981 games with 373 shutouts and 61 no-hitters. Struck out 13,244 batters.

AL LINDE
Pitcher and Outfielder
Home: Midland, Michigan
Elected Hall of Fame: 1958

Background: 20-year career in top competition. Played with five national championship teams—Ke-Nash-A's, Wis. (1934), Deep Rock Oilers, Okla. (1942), Hammer Field Raiders, Calif. (1943–44), Dow Chemical Co., Mich. (1951). Pitched a perfect game for Dow against Caterpillars of Peoria, 1946. Elected to All-American team as both pitcher and outfielder.

Record: Career total 200 no-hit games. 1946: pitched 240 innings and struck out 438 batters. Batted .393 (1951) and .357 (1953) in national tournaments. Playing for Dow Chemical, won 119, lost 39.

JOHN BAKER
Nickname: "Cannonball"
Pitcher
Home: Westport, Connecticut
Elected Hall of Fame: 1961

Background: Started at age 11 as first baseman and outfielder; switched to pitching in junior high. Famed for fast ball. Pitched 4 consecutive no-hit, no-run games in 1938. 26 years of top national competition.

Record: Struck out more than 10,000 batters during career, winning 780, losing 120, with 58 no-hitters. In 4 national tournaments, won 6 games, lost 2.

BETTY EVANS GRAYSON
Nickname: "Bullet Betty"
Pitcher
Home: Portland, Oregon
Elected Hall of Fame: 1959

Background: Played for the boys' team, Glencoe Grade School, and named to city all-star team at 13. Pitched for Erv Lind Florists at 15, won national championship in 1944, holding Phoenix (Ariz.) Ramblers scoreless through 11 innings. Elected to seat in Oregon House of Representatives in 1953 and played for House team against Senate.

Record: Lifetime record, 465 wins and 99 losses with 51 no-hitters and 3 perfect games. Pitched in 5 national championships for Erv Lind Florists. In 1945, pitched 115 consecutive scoreless innings.

M. Marie "Waddy" Wadlow

M. MARIE WADLOW
Nickname: "Waddy"
Pitcher
Home: Peoria, Illinois
Elected Hall of Fame: 1957

Background: Began her softball career with Tabernacle Baptist Church, St. Louis, 1929. Last played with Caterpillar Dieselettes, under coach Chuck McCord, in 1950.

Record: In the national tournament in San Antonio, Texas, in 1950, she pitched 17 innings and gave up only 1 run to the Phoenix Ramblers. Helped the Dieselettes capture 16 straight state championships and 13 titles in West Central Region,

BEN CRAIN
Nickname: "Iron Man"
Pitcher
Home: Omaha, Nebraska
Elected Hall of Fame: 1961

Background: Played Kitten Ball in Iowa at age 11. Once pitched the first game of a double-header right-handed and the second game left-handed. Won citations from the mayor of Omaha and the governor of Nebraska.

Record: Pitched nearly 1,000 games in career, winning 850 with more than 100 no-hitters. Hit more than 300 home runs: .375 lifetime average. Holds record for longest homer in Omaha.

NINA KORGAN
Nickname: "Tiger"
Pitcher
Home: New Orleans, Louisiana
Elected Hall of Fame: 1960

Background: Pitched from 1935–48, winning 6 national championships. Led Higgins Midgets, Tulsa, to title, 1941, pitching 30 innings. Joined Jax Maids, New Orleans, 1942, won 5 national tournaments. Worked in accounting department, Jackson Brewing Company. Height: 5'11". Weight: 180 lbs.

Record: Won 49 of 50 games for local team in first year after high school graduation. In 1941 for Higgins Midgets, she pitched 4 consecutive shutouts, including 1 perfect game. Struck out 20 of 21 batters in national tournament game, 1941.

WARREN GERBER
Nickname: "Fireball"
Pitcher
Home: Cleveland, Ohio
Elected Hall of Fame: 1960

Background: Began national competition with Ferguson State Auditors, Columbus, at age 15. Ferguson finished second in nationals, 1939. Retired 1952. Mayor Anthony Celebreeze of Cleveland proclaimed a "Warren Gerber Day" on June 28, 1960.

Record: Averaged 35 victories per year and 15 strike-outs per game from 1936–52. Pitched 4 perfect games. Lifetime career: 500 wins, with 50 no-hitters.

Amy "Chiefy" Peralta May

AMY PERALTA MAY
Nickname: "Chiefy"
Pitcher
Home: Tempe, Arizona
Elected Hall of Fame: 1957

Background: Full-blooded Indian: first suc-cessful female windmill pitcher. Played with Ramblers of Phoenix, 1938–51. Changed pitching delivery from straight underhand to windmill style. Team captured national championships, 1940, '48, and '49.

Record: Won 35 national tournament games and was named to All-American team 6 times. Pitched more than 500 games, 300 shutouts, and 50 no-hitters. Batted clean-up for Ramblers for 10 years.

CLARENCE MILLER
Nickname: "Buck"
Pitcher
Home: Memphis, Tennessee
Elected Hall of Fame: 1960

Background: Born 1923, played 1940–55 for Buckeye Oil Company and Standard Parts. Exceptional hitter. In 1954 national tournament, Minneapolis, pitched 14-inning game against Washington, struck out 28, and won game with 3-run homer.

Record: Pitched 9 perfect games during career, total of 81 no-hitters. Fanned 21 batters in 1949 exhibition game.

BILL WEST
Pitcher
Home: Ft. Wayne, Indiana
Elected Hall of Fame: 1963

Background: No. 1 pitcher in 10 years with Zollner Pistons. Began with Koelkel Norge, Covington, Ky., in 1938, joined Sixth Ward Boosters, Newport, Ky., 1940. During war, pitched military team to European and Mediterranean championships. 1955, left Zollners to work for General Motors in styling division.

Record: In 1946 and '47, playing for Zollner, had 60 wins, 6 losses against best teams in

U.S. and Canada. Pitched and won 32 games in a row in major competition.

Hugh "Lefty" Johnston

HUGH JOHNSTON
Nickname: "Lefty"
First Base
Home: Orlando, Florida
Elected Hall of Fame: 1961

Background: Born Belfast, Ireland, 1916. Started softball career at age 22. Played with Burr Patterson (1938), Briggs Beautywear (1940), Dow Chemical (1942), and Zollner Pistons, 1943–54.

Record: Helped Pistons win 4 state championships, 4 National Softball League pennants, 2 industrial tournament titles. Lifetime batting average .295. On National Softball League All-Star teams from 1946 through 1953.

BERTHA TICKEY
Nickname: "Blazin' Bertha"
Pitcher
Home: Stratford, Connecticut
Elected Hall of Fame: 1972

Background: Played total of 23 years for championship teams from Orange, Calif., and for Raybestos Brakettes. Ended career, 1968, pitching perfect game against Houston, Tex., and 13-inning no-hit, no-run game against Fresno, Calif. Pitched in first World Championship, 1965, in Melbourne, Australia, losing in finals to Australia, 1–0.

Record: Won 757 and lost 88, hurling 162 no-hit, no-run games. Chosen 18 times for National All-Star Team and 8 times MVP. Holds all-time record for single game strike-outs in national tournaments: struck out 20 in 7 innings in 1953. Pitched 3 perfect games in national tournaments. Recorded 69 wins in national tournaments and pitched 11 championships.

ROBERT FORBES
Outfielder
Home: Clearwater, Florida
Elected Hall of Fame: 1966

Background: Youngest player to join the Clearwater Bombers, at age 14. Led Bombers to victory in 1950, '54, and '56 with powerful hitting.

Record: Surpassed all tournament hitters with .471 average. Elected to All-American team in 1951, '53, and '56.

Kay Rich

KAY RICH
Outfielder-Infielder
Home: Fresno, California
Elected Hall of Fame: 1963

Background: Starting 1938, played with Colton Cuties, Ontario Lionettes, Glendora, Long Beach, Woolworth, Alameda, and Fresno Rockets. 9 years in the Pacific Coast Women's Softball League.

Record: With Betsy Ross Rockets, won national championship 1953 and 1957. Lifetime .312 batting average with 375 hits in 1,201 at-bats. With Rockets, never lost a game in state or regional tournaments.

JOHN HUNTER
Nickname: "Big John"
Pitcher
Home: Clearwater, Florida
Elected Hall of Fame: 1963

Background: Southpaw, slingshot pitcher. In first national appearance, 1950, Austin, Tex., he struck out 16 and gave up 1 hit to beat Portland. In 1953 National Tournament, with bases loaded and no outs, Hunter replaced Herb Dudley on the mound and struck out Midland, Mich., in 9 pitches.

Record: In first 2 years with Clearwater Bombers, won 85 games, lost 6, struck out 1,480 batters. Lifetime record of 275 wins and 19 losses.

TOM CASTLE
First Base
Home: Rochester, New York
Elected Hall of Fame: 1964

Background: Started off in baseball, joined Kodak softball team in 1936, winning National Championships in '36 and '40. Played 25 years. After retirement from Kodak, became umpire for a college baseball, fast- and slow-pitch softball.

Record: Lifetime .340 batting average. Played in nationals 11 times with Kodak Park.

BOBBY SPELL
Pitcher
Home: Lake Charles, Louisiana
Elected Hall of Fame: 1976

Background: Pitched for Clearwater Bombers, Raybestos Cardinals, and teams in the Lake Charles area.

Record: Gave up only 1 earned run in first 159⅔ innings of national tournament competition. Pitched 205½ innings in national competition. Struck out 258 batters: compiled 18–9 record in national tournament play.

Margaret Dobson

MARGARET DOBSON
Third Base
Home: Portland, Oregon
Elected Hall of Fame: 1964

Background: Played with Erv Lind Florists in 1945 after 2 years with Vancouver, Wash. Took part in 9 national tournaments: named to the All-American team in 1949 and '50.

Record: Batted .615 in national tournament, 1950, playing for Erv Lind Florists. Elected to Portland Hall of Fame, 1962.

DONALD RARDIN
Pitcher and Infielder
Home: Lexington, Kentucky
Elected Hall of Fame: 1975

Background: Pitched on championship teams in Open and Industrial Slow-pitch divisions. Started 1956 with Newport, Ky., and played 1965–68 with IBM team of Lexington. Played in more than 2,400 organized softball games.

Record: Lifetime batting average of .606. Pitching record: 234 wins, 39 losses. Named MVP at 1966 National Industrial Tourney. Pitching for IBM, allowed only 13 runs and 40 hits in 6 games.

BILLY WOJIE
Third Base
Home: New Haven, Connecticut
Elected Hall of Fame: 1967

Background: Played for Columbus Auto Body Bears and Raybestos Cardinals. Saved the 1956 tournament, by smashing a home run off a pitch by Johnny Hunter with bases loaded.

Record: Batted .286 in 7 years with Cardinals. Won batting title in 1955 and '56 with .312 and .290 averages. Named to All-New England 6 years, and played in 8 national tournaments. All-American 1955, '59, and '61.

DOT WILKINSON
Catcher
Home: Phoenix, Arizona
Elected Hall of Fame: 1970

Background: Played more than 33 years for the PBSW Ramblers of Phoenix, Ariz., national champions in 1940, '48, and '49. In national tournament in Texas, 1950, she played 43 innings in one day.

Record: Compiled .300 lifetime batting average. Named 19 times to All-American teams.

Sam "Sambo" Elliott

Carolyn Thome Hart

SAM ELLIOTT
Nickname: "Sambo"
Pitcher
Home: Decatur, Georgia
Elected Hall of Fame: 1957

Background: Started playing in 1934 at age
22 and went 21 seasons, appearing in 6 national tournaments. Worked for Western Electric Company and last played for Knowles
Electric of Georgia.

Record: Pitched no-hitter in his first game
and won state championship in first year.
Hurled 1,133 games, won 1,046, and lost 87.
107 no-hitters and 26 perfect games. Totaled
13,936 strike-outs, averaging 12.3 per 7-in-
ning game.

CAROLYN THOME HART
Outfielder
Home: Pekin, Illinois
Elected Hall of Fame: 1966

Background: Learned softball from her father, a semi-pro baseball player, when she was
12. Played for Caterpillar Dieselettes and
Pekin Lettes until 1962.

Record: Lifetime .301 average. Led Pekin in
hitting 3 years; runner-up 4 times. Named to
All-American team 4 years.

NOLAN WHITLOCK
Shortstop
Home: Rossville, Georgia
Elected Hall of Fame: 1967

Background: In 1952 played with Industrial Sales Team of Miami, runners-up in national championships in Stratford. Played for Clearwater Bombers at national championships, 1953–57.

Record: All-American shortstop, 1954; scored winning home run for Bombers. In 1956 hit 2 homers in final game to take National Crown for Bombers.

Roy Stephenson

Nolan Whitlock

ROY STEPHENSON
Pitcher
Home: Muttontown, New York
Elected Hall of Fame: 1965

Background: At age 15 joined employee team on Long Island. Was "added player" with Dejur Cameramen, officially joining team in 1955. Retired, 1960.

Record: Played in 4 state tournaments, compiling 15–2 record, with 40 wins, 3 losses in regionals. Named to All-American teams 5 times and compiled a 23–16 record in national tournaments.

JOHN SPRING
Pitcher
Home: Aurora, Illinois
Elected Hall of Fame: 1970

Background: Played for Briggs Beautyware, Detroit, for Raybestos Cardinals, Aurora Sealmasters, and Ft. Monmouth. Started career at 19 in Little Rock, Ark., pitching no-hitter against Ohio. 1953, he made history at national tournaments, pitching Briggs out of Losers' Bracket to national championship. Pitched 3 games on the final day, winning, 1–0, 2–0, and 1–0.

Record: Lifetime record of 438 wins, 62 losses. Played on 5 national championship teams: won All-Army Championship with Ft. Monmouth, N.J., 1955; went to 17 consecutive national tournaments; All-American 8 times.

CHARLES JUSTICE
Nickname: "Big Justice"
Pitcher
Home: Detroit, Michigan
Elected Hall of Fame: 1974

Background: 6'1", 210 lbs.: played softball for 27 years. Started in Pontiac, Mich., 1936; won National Negro Amateur Softball Championship in 1937. Played with Flint M & S Orange, Toronto's Tip Top Tailors, in the Michigan Chronicle Fastball League (1959–64), and the International Fastball League (1965). Favored windmill pitching and taught in numerous softball clinics.

Record: Lifetime record, 873 wins and 92 losses. Won ASA National Championship with Tip Top Tailors in 1949: team finished second in 1950 with Justice leading in pitching and hitting.

Ruth Sears

RUTH SEARS
First Base
Home: Santa Ana, California
Elected Hall of Fame: 1960

Background: Started 1936 with Green Cat Cafe, Santa Ana City League. Played for Orange Lionettes 1937–55; led team in hitting every year but two. Husband, Chub, coached the Lionettes 1947–55. In 1950 national tourney, she played 26 consecutive innings to win first national title.

Record: .267 national tourney batting average, with lifetime record of .425. Batted .585 with Orange in first season.

JIM CHAMBERS
Nickname: "Big Jim"
Pitcher
Home: Oshkosh, Wisconsin
Elected Hall of Fame: 1966

Background: Played in Aurora, Ill., and led Chicago Match Corporation to second place in 2 national tournaments. Pioneer in sling-shot pitching. After retirement, became commissioner of the Lakeshore Fast Pitch League.

Record: Struck out 43 men during one game at national tournament in 1946. Career record of 4,380 strike-outs with 209 no-hitters.

LITTLE-KNOWN FACTS

Stronger Than the Pen

A sportswriter for the Chicago *Daily News* went out to do a story on the new professional softball team, the Chicago Storm, and never came back. He tried out for the position of pitcher and made the team.

Second Time Around

In a softball game in Iowa, a pitcher threw two strikes with a sizzling fast ball. The third pitch was a slow ball. The batter took a quick swing, missed the ball, then continued around, hitting a home run on the second swing.

Always a Gamble

In 1947 and '48 the "croupiers" of Harold's Gambling Club in Reno won the Nevada State Championship.

Teeth in Softball

A frequent winner of Chicago's 16-inch slow-pitch championship is Dr. Carlucci's Bobcats. Every year, Dr. Carlucci gets a letter from the local dental association with a reprimand for advertising his dental practice through his team. The letter usually includes a note of congratulations for winning the national championships again.

Rookie Star

Henry Winkler, star of *Happy Days,* became pitcher for the ABC team, the Dreaded Ten, only 2 years after he learned to play softball. Ron Howard is the team's shortfielder and MVP.

Lone Star Singers

In the 1936 National Tournament the girls from Wichita Falls, Texas, played in bare feet and sang Texan songs between innings.

Wicked Windmill

The first windmill pitch ever seen in softball was at a picnic game in Detroit in 1922. It was thrown by Mike Lutomski, a school principal, and was declared illegal by Hubert Johnson, the unofficial rules boss in Detroit. So many playground kids adopted the windmill style that Johnson had to reverse his decision and declare it legal in 1926.

Free Charity

When Louis Delmastro, a pitcher for Pittsburgh, won the award for Most Valuable Player in the nationals at Parma, Ohio, he was almost overcome with emotion. He took off his hat, his jersey, shoes, and glove, and gave them all to a crippled child who was sitting on the side lines. The only trouble was . . . the glove and shoes belonged to another player.

Mets Play Penguins
In an annual series of softball games, members of the Metropolitan Opera Company (Mets) play against musicians from the New York Philharmonic. The orchestra team is called The Penguins.

Bumbling Babe

Babe Ruth once umpired a championship softball game in New York, and agreed to do a demonstration after the game. Unfortunately, the softball pitcher unleashed 5 fast balls. Babe swung at all of them . . . and missed.

On the last pitch, he retrieved the ball from the catcher and slammed it into the distant bleachers.

"I just wanted to see if that big ball could be hit," he said, as he strode away from the batter's box.

Fire the Ump

In the 1947 World Championship between Tony Piet's Pontiac Queens and the Jax Brewers, a robust female pitcher named Frieda Savona protested strenuously to an umpire's calls. He was thrown out of the tournament.

Triple-K-League

In 1957 a team from the Ku Klux Klan won the city championship in Chattanooga, Tennessee. The team was beaten in the state finals.

Stealing Allowed

In 1974, the New York City Police played a team of ex-convicts, all members of the Fortune Society, for the benefit of One-to-One, an organization that helps retarded children. The pitcher for the Fortune Society insisted on base stealing so the cops couldn't nap on the job. But the police won anyway, 12–4.

Nucleus of a Team

In 1957 the atomic scientists of Los Alamos formed their own softball team to play in local competition.

Bomber on First

Joe Louis, the boxing champ, belonged to a softball team called Joe Louis' Brown Bombers. He played first base.

Conclusion

SOFTBALL GONE BY

When does someone decide that softball is going to be part of his or her life? For most softballers, I suspect, it's just a matter of doing what comes naturally. A kid finds out he can pitch pretty well, and soon he's practicing every day, getting hints from the experts around town. A softballer goes up to bat and discovers the indescribable pleasure that comes from making a solid hit. I mean a *solid* hit, the kind where you look at the ball floating toward outer space and say to yourself, "I can't believe it. *I did that?*" If you don't watch out, you'll be coming back for more—every afternoon, evening, or weekend. Just to hit that ball and make it soar. To catch it, on-the-run, for a third out. To throw it home before the runner slides in. Pitch, hit, catch, throw—it's all the game. But if you once experience that insidious all-American thrill, you're liable to get caught—who knows how, who knows why—in the love of that game.

Just being there has immeasurable value, and that's one reason why so many people come to watch. Fans yell and argue and wave their fists in the air. They call the players good names and bad. They shriek like banshees and voice their expert opinions like Howard Cosell. When they arrive at the field, they have the pushiness of anticipation and when they go home, they have the cool smugness of people who can say, "I saw it happen."

To families in small towns all around the country, softball is an excuse to spend hot summer evenings by a grassy field. People watch old friends and young rookies play on unheralded teams in unheard-of leagues. Hits and runs are scored around the dusty diamond. Reputations rise and fall in the sultry air that hangs over the field. But there's a chance of a breeze in the late afternoon, and the all-stars from Vidalia have a chance of beating the all-stars from Macon for the first time in ten years. That's worth staying to watch.

In the city, softball is a presence that creeps into midtown offices, hangs around the water cooler, adds zest to a lunch-time conversation, and sneaks down the corridor and out the door long before five o'clock. The manager has a glove in the bottom drawer of the desk. The secretary has T-shirt and sneakers in the closet. The vice-president has a photograph on his wall of a mighty softball slugger—himself.

Once you take your place on the softball field, you don't have to worry about anything for the next seven innings of your life. Just think about the play, the batter, the players on base. Straighten your hat and forget any troubles you might have had before the game. Forty-two outs later, you can go home and start worrying and griping and giving yourself ulcers. But out there, you're allowed to forget that business—and that's okay, because the softball field is a special place.

Then there's your team. You get to know the strengths and weaknesses of those people, their temperaments and capabilities. One of the most important (and least noted) rules in softball is this: You can't change teams in the middle of the game. You know what that means? That means you've got to live with those players for at least seven innings and maybe a whole season. Like it or not, you're stuck with them.

Softball friendships are frequently valuable and long-lasting. If someone hits a home run while you're on first, you don't forget about him right away. All the yelling, hand-shaking, and backslapping are sincere—you can't fake it, and no one would try. Teams change, fielders age, and an entire season is reduced to a mere blip on the oscilloscope of softball history. There are the sentiments that go with winning a championship, and there are the understandings that develop, oddly enough, through long-standing rivalry. There's also beer after the game, jokes, stories, eloquent recollections, and the promise of a better season to come.

So here's the formula. Get yourself a bat, a ball, a glove, and a hat with a big brim. A supply of hotdogs and the beverage of your choice. Find twenty people, give or take a dozen, with the same idea in mind. A big field with three bases, home plate, and a backstop. A bunch of friends to shout encouragement. And you're ready to play softball for just about the rest of your life.

Good luck!

Words to Play With

ALL-IMPORTANT SOFTBALL TERMS

Appeal play—An appeal is called when the team in the field claims that there has been a violation of the rules by the team at bat. The four appeal plays are: (1) batting out of order, (2) leaving a base before a fly ball is touched, (3) not touching a base or touching out of order, (4) overrunning first base and then being tagged on the attempt to go to second. An appeal must be made by the defensive team and called by the umpire before the next pitch or before the defensive team has left the field.

Assist—A fielder who helps make a play that puts a runner out is credited with an assist.

Base on balls—A walk as a result of four balls being called on the batter.

Base path—The "running lane" 3 feet on either side of the base line. A runner may not swerve out of this lane to avoid being tagged, but he may step out of the path to avoid collision or interference.

Base runner—In fast pitch, the base runner is allowed to lead off the base before the pitch or to steal during the pitch. In slow pitch, the runner must keep contact with the base until the pitched ball reaches home plate or is hit. If he runs early, the runner is out and "no pitch" is declared.

Batter—Must take his position within the lines of the batter's box and must avoid interference with the catcher.

Batting average—A figure obtained by dividing a player's total number of base hits by total times at bat. Sacrifice hits, free bases, and walks are not considered times at bat in figuring out this average.

Batting order—Sequence in which the team players come to bat. Batting order remains the same throughout the game, except when a player is replaced by a pinch hitter.

Behind on the count—The pitcher is "behind on the count" when he's thrown more balls than strikes; the batter is behind with more strikes than balls.

Blocked ball—Declared when a non-player touches the ball, or when it hits something that isn't part of the equipment on the field. It automatically becomes a dead ball.

Box score—Number of runs, hits, and errors at the end of the game for each team.

Bunt—A ball tapped to the infield with the bat held between both hands—allowed only in fast pitch. A "bluff bunt" is when the batter assumes a bunting stance but doesn't attempt to hit the ball. With a "sacrifice bunt" the batter is out, but another runner advances or scores.

Catch—A player must catch the ball with hands or glove. It's not a legal catch if he prevents the ball from falling to the ground with his body or clothing, or collides with another player and drops the ball.

Charged conference—Occurs when the team in the field requests a suspension of play so that the manager (or other player) can confer with the pitcher. Only one charged conference per inning is allowed. If there is a second conference, the pitcher must be removed from the game.

Chopped ball—In slow pitch, an illegal hit. The batter strikes downward with a chopping motion of the bat to make the ball take a hard bounce.

Clean-up batter—Number four in the batting order.

Coach—A member of the team at bat who stands in the coach's box by first or third to direct the players of his team in running the bases. Two coaches allowed.

Cutoff player—An infielder who gets into position to intercept a throw from the outfield.

Dead ball—After a play has been made, the ball is technically "dead" until the pitcher is in position again and the umpire has called, "Play ball."

Defensive team—The team in the field.

Dislodged base—A base moved from its proper position. The runner is not penalized for a dislodged base, and he is not expected to tag a base that is far out of position.

ERA—"Earned run average." An earned run is charged to a pitcher every time a runner reaches home plate by safe hits, sacrifices, walks, and (in fast pitch) stolen bases. To figure out the ERA, multiply the number of earned runs charged to a pitcher by seven and divide by the number of innings the pitcher was on the field.

Fair ball—Any ball that falls on or between the first- or third-base foul lines, which extend all the way to the fence in right and left field. A ball is fair if it passes over any part of fair territory on its way to the outfield. Also fair if the ball hits first or third base or if it touches any player or umpire in fair territory. To be a home run, the ball must go over the fence in fair territory.

Fielder's choice—When a player in the field has a choice between throwing to first or to another base, he may make a "fielder's choice" to put out a runner.

Fly ball—Any ball batted into the air. The batter is out if a fly ball is caught by a defensive player.

Force out—To put out a runner by touching the next base when the runner is forced to advance.

Foul ball—A batted ball that settles on foul territory or passes first or third base in foul territory. The ball is foul if it touches an umpire or player in foul territory.

Foul tip—A ball that is "tipped" by the batter and held by the catcher. If the foul tip doesn't go higher than the batter's head and is caught, a strike is called.

Full count—A count of three balls and two strikes against the batter.

Ground ball—A batted ball that rolls or bounces along the ground.

Home team—The team in whose field the game is played. The home team always begins in the field at the bottom of the first inning, with the visiting team at bat.

Illegally batted ball—It's illegal when the batter's foot is completely outside of the box or touching home plate, or when he uses an illegal bat. The batter is out, and if he uses an illegal bat, he's suspended from the game.

Illegally caught ball—A ball caught in the mask, cap, or clothing of a player. Base runners are allowed three free bases on a batted ball, two on a thrown ball, and a home run if the illegally caught ball would have cleared the fence.

Infield—The portion of the field included within the lines of the diamond or covered by infielders playing their normal positions.

Infield fly—A fair-hit fly ball that can be easily handled by an infielder. If a batter hits an infield fly with runners on first and second, or on first, second, and third with less than two out, the batter is immediately out. This is called the "infield fly rule."

Inning—A full inning has been played when both teams have had a turn at bat.

Interference—Any attempt to hinder or obstruct a player on the other team during play. The player charged with interference is out.

Lead off—To move off the base before the ball is pitched. Allowed only in fast pitch.

Legal touch—The runner may be touched by the hand or glove holding the ball. It is not a legal touch if the ball is juggled or dropped by the fielder after he has touched the runner.

Line drive—A hard-hit fly ball that stays low to the ground.

Obstruction—Called when a fielder who is not holding or fielding the ball stands in the way of a base runner. If obstruction occurs during play, the runner is awarded a free base, and all other runners may advance one base.

Offensive team—The team at bat.

Outfield—The portion of the field outside the first, second, and third base lines.

Overrun or overslide—The player runs beyond the base. At first base, the player is safe on an overrun as long as he doesn't head for second. On all other bases, the runner can be tagged out on an overrun or overslide.

Overthrow—On a throw to a base, the ball goes into foul territory. If the ball is blocked—goes into the dugout or stands—the runners may advance only two bases.

Passed ball—In fast pitch, a pitched ball that should have been caught by the catcher but gets away from him. Base runners can steal on a passed ball.

Perfect game—A game in which the pitcher allows no hits, no runs, and no players on base.

Pick-off—In fast pitch, an attempt to put out a player who is making a steal.

Pinch hitter—A substitute batter. Once a player has been replaced by a pinch hitter, that player is out for the remainder of the game.

Pivot foot—The pitcher must keep the pivot foot in constant contact with the pitching plate until the ball is released. A ball is called if he fails to do so.

Protest—A protest may be made by either team, but only in cases where a playing rule has been misinterpreted, or the correct rule has not been applied by the umpire, or when the correct penalty has not been imposed for a violation.

Pull hitter—A batter who hits the ball hard to the "near" field; e.g., left field for a right-handed hitter. Usually the player is swinging early on the pitch.

Quick-return pitch—An illegal pitch made by the pitcher with the obvious intention of trying to catch the batter off balance. The umpire will declare that "no pitch" has been made.

RBI—"Runs batted in." The batter is credited with an RBI when a run is scored from his hit, sacrifice, or walk.

Sacrifice hit or fly—The batter makes a sacrifice hit so that other runners can advance or score even though he is put out.

Shake off—The pitcher refuses to throw the type of pitch signaled to him by the catcher.

Shutout—The pitcher earns a "shutout" when the other team does not score at any time during the game.

Squeeze play—In fast pitch only. The runner from third tries to steal home when the batter attempts to bunt.

Stealing—The runner may attempt to steal a base during any pitch to a batter. Allowed in fast pitch only.

Strike zone—Differs in fast pitch and slow pitch. In fast pitch, the strike zone is over home plate, between the batter's armpits and the top of his knees. In slow pitch, it's between the batter's highest shoulder and his knees.

Tag-up—On a fly ball the runner must return to base or "tag-up" and may run only after the ball has been touched by a fielder. If he runs without tagging up, he may be put out or called out on an appeal play.

Time—Only the umpire can call "time-out" in order to suspend play. Players must request "time" from the umpire.

Wild pitch—In fast pitch, a pitched ball so wide, low, or high that it can't be handled easily by the catcher.

ABOUT THE AUTHOR

The author (left) and bearded friend (John Warthen) take a break from their hectic spring workout in Vidalia, Georgia, to pose for a few passing crickets. Note the atypical "dress down" uniform of the author, who has adapted the casual style of the seventies to the diamond. During his career as a softball buff, Edward Claflin ("Killer Ed," to his friends) never hit a ball within ten feet of the outfield fence; never took part in a successful double-play; never made it to third base when there was any conceivable way of being put out at second; and never made up his mind which position he was supposed to play. In spite of this remarkable lifetime record, he remains passionately devoted to the sport, which some people find quite alarming. His other interests include sailing, skiing, and watching the grass grow between cracks in the sidewalk during those long summer days when there's not much else to do.